BRANSON
HIKING TRAILS

"COME SEE THE OTHER SIDE OF BRANSON"

FIRST EDITION

BY

BOB AND JANET GARD

GARD HOUSE PUBLISHING

BRANSON MISSOURI

Published by Gard House Publishing
1440 State Highway 248
Suite Q-109
Branson, Mo. 65616
1.417.334.4450
1.866.461.5972

Library of Congress Control Number: 2005939147

ISBN-13:978-0-9773390-0-6
ISBN-10: 0-9773390-0-9

Printed in the United States of America
by RJ Communications, LLC
(BooksJustBooks)

THANK YOU

To everyone who gave us encouragement and support in the writing of this book. We have many friends and family that helped us in one way or another, again, thanks! But there are those that we would like to give special thanks for their guidance, suggestions, time and information. They are:

Cindy Shook – Cindy is the Director of the Branson Parks and Recreation Department and even though very busy was always available to answer our many questions. If she didn't have the answer she knew who to contact.

Larry Van Gilder – Larry is the Director of Branson Public Works. He provided us with information on the history of the stone stairs on the Stairway Trail and the cave on the Old Soldier's Cave Trail. Both of these trails are in the Lakeside Forest Wilderness Area.

Mel & Liz Bilbo – For business advice, ideas, suggestions and the selling and promotion of our book in their store, T. Charleston's Books and Gifts, located in the Grand Village Shops on highway 76.

Craig Erickson – Owner of Downhill Bikes, who shares our view that we need more hiking and biking trails in the Branson area. He has been instrumental in working with the area communities in planning and development of an area wide trail system.

Our Website, *hikebranson.com*

On our website we have pictures that we have taken while hiking the trails listed in the book. There are pictures of animals, insects, scenery and flowers. If you find one that you would like to have you can purchase it through the website. We have historical information and links to area businesses. If there is something that you would like to see on our website or a question that you would like answered, let us know. We will do our best to help. You will notice that we have listed each trail or group of trails by number. By using the table below you will be able to tell what pictures goes with each trail number.

Trail #1	Boston Ferry Road Trail
Trail #2	Stockstill Park Walking Trail
Trail #3	Red, Yellow, and Silver Trails
Trail #4	Purple, White, and Orange Trails
Trail #5	Bear Cave Trail
Trail #6	Old Soldier's Cave Trail
Trail #7	Picnic Trail, Stairway Trail
Trail #8	Chinquapin, Juniper, and Table Rock Lakeshore Trails
Trail #9	Fire Tower Trail
Trail #10	Empire Park Trail
Trail #11	Dewey Bald, Glade, Streamside and Homesteader's Trails
Trail #12	White River Corridor, Canebrake, Fisherman's and White River Bluff Trails

Hope you enjoy our site and come back often. When you contact one of the merchants listed in the book or the website be sure and let them know that Bob and Janet sent you!

TABLE OF CONTENTS

E = Easy   M = Moderate   D = Difficult
For more details of the rating system see page 20.

INTRODUCTION

Welcome to Branson! The live entertainment capitol of the world! For most people, who come to Branson, it is all about the music shows. With around 50 theaters and over 100 different shows there is something for everyone. There are so many shows that if you saw three shows per day, it would take you over a month to see them all! Wow! You better get busy!

The Branson of today is quite a contrast to the Branson that many of us "old timers" remember. There was a time in Branson when the "tourist" season began the first of May and ended in late October. During the winter you could drive down highway 76 and may not even see a car!

Today, Branson is a bustling community. In fact, the busiest time of year is the Christmas season which starts around the first of November and goes through the end of December. There are beautiful Christmas light displays all around town. Colorful lights line the streets, buildings, trees, even the utility poles. With music shows featuring Christmas themes, three discount malls and 50 restaurants offering mouth watering cuisine, it is difficult to decide what is the best part of Christmas in Branson. If you have never been here during the Christmas season you need to come and enjoy the season with us.

Even though the many attractions are a great way to spend your time while on vacation, it wasn't the attractions that originally brought people to the area. It was the natural beauty of the Ozark Mountain hills, rivers, and the great outdoors. Before any dams were ever built, the White River flowed free from the hills in Arkansas, through Missouri, back into Arkansas and finally into the Mississippi River. At that time people came to Branson to float the river and try their hand at catching a large stringer of fish. One of the great float and fishing guides of the area was Jim Owens. People came from the world over to have Jim take them on a float trip down the White River.

In 1907, after the publication of Harold Bell Wright's book,

The Shepherd of the Hills, which was based on the people in these Ozark Mountain Hills, things began to change. People came from all around to see the sites that were mentioned in the book. The Shepherd of the Hills Farm which is located on highway 76, between Branson and Silver Dollar City, still has an outdoor play based on the book. Then in 1913, upstream from the town of Forsyth, the first dam on the White River, Powersite, was completed. This was the first man made lake in the central United States and people came to fish and swim in its warm waters. The main reason that the dam was built was to supply something that was new to the area, electricity! Today, it is hard to imagine a world without it, but back then it was a novelty. Even with the building of the dam, it would be years before most people in the area had access to electrical power. Bill Large, a friend of ours, says he remembers helping his dad wire houses and barns for electricity back in the 1940's and that some people didn't understand how the same electricity could heat up a stove and cool down a refrigerator! My how things have changed! By the way, Bill grew up on a farm along the White River that was located about one mile north of the present Long Creek Bridge on highway 86 and is now under about 150 feet of water.

With the completion of Table Rock Dam in 1958 Table Rock Lake was formed. Lake Taneycomo (which gets its name from Taney county Missouri, _Taney_ _co_unty _mo_) was now a cold water lake and too cold for swimming and the fishing had changed forever. Along with the dam, a fish hatchery was built to raise and stock trout for the cold waters of the new lake. Today, Lake Taneycomo is well known for its excellent trout fishing and people come here year round to try and catch the big one!

There are two other dams that have been built on the White River, both are located in Arkansas. Bulls Shoals Dam, located on the lower end, was completed in 1947 and Beaver Dam, which was built on the upper end of the White River, was completed in 1960.

Today, Branson truly is blessed with many activities from which to choose. Just to name a few of the things that you can do while you are in Branson, you can see a music show, eat at a fine restaurant, go shopping, swimming, water skiing, diving, fishing, floating, golfing, hunting, hiking, parasailing, bike riding, ride a go cart, take a helicopter ride, hot air balloon rides, see a movie, tour a cave, visit a theme park, a water park, and you can even ride a Duck! Whew! And all of this can be done in or within a few minutes of Branson. For more information on some of these activities see the next section, **Branson Activities**.

Today, Branson is host to several million people a year but it hasn't always been like this. The town of Branson was founded in 1903 and incorporated on April 1, 1912 with 1,200 residents. Soon there were hotels and a resort on the river front along with an ice plant, a soft drink bottling plant, an ice cream factory and a candy factory. The warm waters of the newly formed Lake Taneycomo were starting to bring people to this out of the way place.

By the 1930's Branson had a reputation as an inexpensive vacation destination. A lot of people were coming by trains and cars, even though the roads were not the best in the world. The road between Branson and Springfield, at that time, was nothing more than a path that wound its way through the Ozark hills for 75 miles, with no place to pass! That's a far cry from the forty mile, four lane highway that we have today. But even though it wasn't the easiest place to get to, the people still came. It was that kind of popularity that helped Branson to survive the Depression years.

In 1949, two men, Steve Miller and Joe Todd came up with the idea of putting up a large lighted Adoration Scene on top of the bluff at Mount Branson, across Lake Taneycomo from downtown Branson. With the help of other folks in town they built and erected the scene's figures, some as tall as 28 feet. Then on the first Sunday of December the lights of the Adoration scene were turned on for all to see. This tradition still continues today. Every year, at dusk, on the first Sunday of December, as many as 30,000 people gather in downtown Branson to see the Adoration scene lit up and watch the night time parade.

In 1957, along the lakefront, the Mabe family started entertaining visitors with their music on the weekends. They became known as the Baldknobbers, named for a vigilante group that roamed these hills in the late 1800's. Soon afterwards, the Presley family, who had a farm way out on highway 76, built a metal building and started to entertain visitors with their music. Today, the Presley family still entertains visitors at the same location. The Baldknobber show didn't move out on highway 76 until later. That is why you will hear the Baldknobbers say they, "started it all" as the first music show in Branson while the Presley's say they were the first show on highway 76, now known as "the strip". There have been many different shows that have come and gone over the years but these two shows have survived because of their talent and dedication to good, clean family entertainment.

The music industry continued to grow and for many years it seemed to over shadow the other activities found in and around Branson. Music shows are still quite popular but many people are looking to getting back to what originally brought people to Branson in the first place. They want to enjoy the beautiful Ozark Mountain Hills and "Come See the Other Side of Branson" by doing things like shop, golf, fish, swim, bike and even hike! A lot of the people that are coming to Branson are from the "baby boom" generation and I believe we are staying more active and trying to stay in shape as we get older. I say "we" because Janet and I are part of that generation. That is why we have included "calories burned" in the information of each trail. That way you will know how far you have to hike so you can eat that dessert and not gain weight! See how thoughtful we are!

There is a long range plan to connect area communities with 82 miles of hiking and biking trails. The first phase has already started. It is a 10 foot wide asphalt trail from Skaggs Community Health Center to Stockstill Park. Branson has also announced that they have immediate plans of adding to and extending trails within the Branson Park system. This is exciting news so be sure and check our website for updates.

BRANSON ACTIVITIES

Below is just a brief list of some of the activities that you can do while you are in Branson. For more information and links where you can find information concerning what is going on in the Branson area please visit our website.

The first thing you need to do when you get to Branson is to stop at almost any gas station, convenience store or restaurant for a free map of the Branson area. There are many side roads off of highway 65 and 76 that will help you get around and avoid some of the traffic while you are here in Branson. If you are already here in Branson go by the Chamber of Commerce located on highway 248 just west of highway 65 or some of the information sites around town. Take note, that some of these "Branson Information" places will try to get you to tour their timeshare properties, whether you go or not is up to you, but they will give you a free map of the area and help answer your questions.

MUSIC SHOWS

One of the first things people ask us is, "What is the best show to see?" That is a hard question to answer because all the shows are good and it is just a matter of what type of music and entertainment that you like. There is old country, new country, comedy, acrobats, fiddle playing, gospel, western, big band, 50's & 60's, rock and roll, pop, Broadway and variety shows, you name it and we are sure to have it. There are shows that have been here in Branson for several years and then there are others that may have been here only a few weeks. Some are here year round and others come in for special engagements. You can always ask the people at the motel, restaurant, or gas station what they would recommend. There are also free visitor magazines that you can pick up at different business around town that have maps and information on area activities.

MOVIES

I remember a time when the only movie theatre in town was the old Owen theatre on Commercial Street in downtown Branson. The building is still there today and being used for music shows. But if you would like to see a movie there is the I-Max theater on Shepherd of the Hills Parkway just east of highway 76 on the west side of town. They have one large I-Max screen that show the I-Max films and three other screens that show the latest releases. Often on the big I-Max screen they will show a regular movie and that is quite an experience to see and hear. There is no home entertainment system that can compare to the sound of an I-Max system, so be sure and go. For more information call 417.335.4832.

The other movie house that shows the latest releases is Branson Meadows Cinema, located at the Factory Shops at Branson Meadows, it has 11 screens, and is located on Gretna road about one mile west of highway 248. Give them a call at 417.332.2884.

SHOPPING

There are a variety of things from which to choose that will keep everyone occupied while here in Branson. One of those is SHOPPING! There are three discount malls that attract a lot of attention, Tanger, Factory Merchants (Red Roof), and Factory Shops at Branson Meadows. There a hundreds of other smaller stores, craft shops and flea markets around the area that provide a variety of merchandise and create that unique shopping experience. The I-Max Theatre Complex has several shops and places to eat. Historic Downtown Branson along with the newly opened Branson Landing, on the shore of Lake Taneycomo, will provide enough shops to keep you busy all day.

One place that you must visit while here in Branson is the Grand Village. It is located on highway 76 by the Grand Palace. There are 26 unique specialty shops along the cobblestone streets. Friends of ours, Mel and Liz, own and operate the Reflections Thomas Kinkade Signature Gallery, Kringles

Christmas Store, T. Charleston's Books and Gifts and Mel's Hard Luck Diner. The Kinkade store has beautiful paintings and prints of the famous artist, Thomas Kinkade and just stepping into Kringles, the huge Christmas store, makes you feel like its December no matter what time of year you are there. Like books? Go to the T. Charleston's store and check out the large selection of books they have on many different subjects. Here you will be able to find a lot of the local books from the area, including ours! If Mel and Liz don't have it they can get it for you. Then there is Mel's Hard Luck Diner, a truly unique dining experience. I know, when you think of shopping a restaurant doesn't usually come to mind but you do have to eat and they do sell music CD's! What makes this place such an unusual dining experience is that the servers sing to you as you eat your meal! Be sure and check out these places while you are here, and if you see Mel or Liz, tell them Bob and Janet sent you!

THEME PARKS, CAVES, CRAFTS AND PLAYS

The most notable theme park in the area is without a doubt, Silver Dollar City. It has grown over the years and has received many awards. But did you know that it started out as a cave tour? In 1889 a man by the name of William Henry Lynch purchased Marvel Cave and one square mile of land around it for $10,000. The cave was opened in 1894 but soon had to close due to lack of money. After raising more capitol the cave was reopened sometime after 1900 and has remained open ever since. When Mr. Lynch died in 1927 the cave stayed in the family until it was purchased by Hugo Herschend, a Chicago vacuum cleaner salesman, around 1932. Hugo passed away about five years later so, Mary his wife and two sons, Jack and Pete started managing the business. They began to make improvements to the cave which included a train that would take visitors up 218 feet back to the top of the cave. Wanting to do something to attract even more visitors they decided to build a frontier town on the land around the entrance to the cave. With a main street, a church, log cabin and five shops

Silver Dollar City was underway. Each day, on the main street, to entertain the guests that were waiting to tour the cave, there was a reenactment of the feud between the Hatfields and McCoys. From those humble beginnings the Herschend family has made Silver Dollar City into the great amusement park and craft show it is today.

Celebration City, also owned by Silver Dollar City, it is your late afternoon and evening place to be. With rides, arcades, a laser light show and fireworks after dark. It is located on highway 376 just west of highway 76 on the west end of Branson.

Shepherd of the Hills Farm is where the characters of the Shepherd of the Hills book, written by Harold Bell Wright, come to life. Since, August 6, 1959, the play, based on the book, has been performed under the stars making it the longest running outdoor drama ever. During the day you can visit the log cabins, wagons and crafts of yesteryear. You can also go up 230 feet to the top of Inspiration Tower and enjoy spectacular views of the Ozark Hills.

There are several places around town that make and sell crafts. The bigger ones are Silver Dollar City, Shepherd of the Hills, Engler Block, located on highway 76 about one mile west of highway 65, and Coffelt Country on highway 165 about a mile south of west highway 76. There are several flea markets that sell all types of craft items.

WATER PARKS

In the summer White Water is a popular place to go, especially if you have children. They have all kinds of water rides, a lazy river for floating, a wave pool and a little kid's area. Back in the good old days, before Branson had expanded out this far, the area to the east of highway 76 (to the right if you are coming from downtown Branson) between the Lodge of the Ozarks and White Water, was the location of the Branson Airport. It was the flattest piece of land we had in this area and what did they do? Brought in truck load after truck load of dirt and built up mounds for the water rides! Now I ask, wouldn't it have been easier and less expensive if they had used the side of one of the many hills that were already here?

The city of Branson has opened up a recreation area on the Branson Hills Parkway about 1.8 miles west of highway 65 called the RecPlex. While the water park is not as big as White Water it is less expensive, so if you want to save a few dollars, be sure and check it out. For more information call 417.337.8510.

WATER ACTIVITIES

If the water parks are not for you maybe one of the lakes will do. There is Table Rock Lake, Lake Taneycomo and Bull Shoals Lake where there is boating, skiing, swimming, snorkeling, diving, parasailing, fishing, sunbathing, floating, cruising, and riding a duck, did I leave anything out? I am sure I did but you get the point, there are a lot of things you can do in and on the area waters.

You might wonder about the cruising and riding a duck. Well, the Showboat Branson Belle is a large boat docked on highway 265, at the State Park by Table Rock Dam that takes you on lake cruises. They will provide you with a show and something to eat while you cruise on the water.

And riding a duck is easier than you might think. No, we are not talking about riding a bird; we are talking about riding an amphibious water craft that takes you on a tour of the area on both land and water. If you are new to the area and don't know the streets very well this is a great way to see the sites, hear some history about the area and learn your way around. And besides that, you get a wacky quacker! In case you don't know what that is, it is a whistle that when you blow it sounds like a duck. Just think, it will give the kids something to do when you get back in the car, or your motel room!

If you want to swim a good place to go is Moonshine Beach located just north of Table Rock Dam by the new spillway. It cost just a few dollars a carload but is does have sand on the beach, which around here is a treat, because for the most part, if you haven't noticed, we grow rocks.

If diving is what you are interested in be sure and see Louis Chapman at Scuba Sports located in Branson on highway 248. They are Southwest Missouri's only PADI 5-Star IDC Center. They are very knowledgeable and will be glad to help you with classes, tours, rentals, equipment sales and service. Their phone number is 417.334.9073 and the website is scuba-sports.com.

Maybe what you would like to do is catch a rainbow or brown trout. We have the solution; visit the River Run Outfitters owned by Stan and Carolyn Parker. They have a full line fly shop and guide service offering western style drift fishing on Lake Taneycomo. Their store is located on highway 165, just up the hill from the Table Rock Dam fish hatchery. You can give them a call at 417.332.0460, toll free 877-699-FISH (3474), or their website at riverrunoutfitters.com.

BIKING

Janet and I have started doing some bike riding and have really enjoyed it. Now, we are not experts by any means. We still like our trails fairly level and not too rough. The Table Rock Lakeshore Trail is one of our favorites. It is paved, level and just the way we like it. The RecPlex Trails are also paved trails that are level.

For those of you that like to bike cross country the Busiek State Forest Trails are good places for natural trails that go up and down hills and across creeks. For more information on biking trails in the area go and see our friend Craig at Down Hill Bikes. He can help you with gear, equipment, repairs and point you in the right direction for the trails of your skill level. Give him a call at 417.335.4455, or visit his website at downhillbikes.biz.

PHOTOGRAPHY

Taking pictures is a great way of capturing the beauty of the Ozarks and keeping memories of your visit to the Branson area. Whether you have an instamatic or one of the new digital cameras be sure and take it along with you wherever you go.

If you need someone to take wedding pictures, family portraits, passport photos, class reunion pictures, etc. then you need to stop by and see Lori or James. Maybe you need camera supplies, have prints made or just some advice then go by and visit them at the Koi Garden Plaza on highway 76 just west of highway 65. Give them a call at 417.337.5747 or visit their website at *bransonphoto.com*.

OTHER ACTIVITIES

We have mentioned just a few of the activities that take place in and around the Branson area throughout the year. There are also parades, craft shows, concerts, car shows, festivals, fishing tournaments and many other events that you can enjoy during your stay in the Branson area.

Branson is a very patriotic community that wants to pay honor and tribute to the veteran's that have served our country. There are events held at different times of the year to show how much we appreciate the service and sacrifice that so many have made to keep our country free.

For more information on these and other activities taking place throughout the year you can contact the different Chamber's of Commerce in the area.

Branson Chamber of Commerce   417.334.4084
Hollister Chamber of Commerce   417.334.3050
Forsyth Chamber of Commerce   417.546.2741
Table Rock Lake Area C of C   417.739.2564

HIKING

There are a lot of interesting and beautiful things to see while you are in Branson, but Janet and I believe that if you want to see the real beauty of Branson you need to hike the many trails found in the Ozark Mountain hills. This will allow you to see its natural beauty up close and personal. Before we begin, there are some items we need to go over that, hopefully, will make your hiking safer and more enjoyable.

WHAT TO WEAR

The most important thing is to make sure you are comfortable. You need to have a good pair of shoes that fit correctly and are not too tight or too loose. If your shoes cause a blister your time hiking will not be enjoyable. If you are using the paved walking trails a good pair of walking tennis shoes may be all you need, But, if you plan on hiking the many natural trails where there are hills, rock ledges, loose rooks and creeks we suggest that you invest in a good pair of hiking shoes that support your ankles. They are well worth the investment because it allows you to spend your time enjoying the trails with its beautiful scenery instead of thinking about your aching feet.

In the spring, summer and early fall hiking shorts are what most people wear, although long pants that are light weight and not too tight would be ok. Of course, during cold weather you will want to wear long pants to help keep warm. When it is cold you will want to dress in layers so that you do not become too hot and sweat. Wet clothes in winter time can cause you to chill and get cold.

A good hat is always nice. In the summer a light colored straw hat will help keep the hot sun off your head and out of your eyes. In the winter a heavier hat will help keep the heat from your body from escaping help keep you warm. I have a leather hat that I like to wear when it is cold and it also does a good job of keeping the rain off my head.

A good pair of sunglasses is good to take along on those

sunny days no matter what time of the year it is.

WHAT TO TAKE

Take only what you need. The trails that are listed in this book are mainly day hikes that can be hiked in an hour or two with the longest being about six hours. For the shorter hikes all you will need maybe your camera, water to drink and a few snack bars.

For the longer hikes we take a backpack full of supplies. Since you never know what you will need I always try to be prepared. In my backpack I keep my camera supplies, a small first aid kit, a couple of ponchos, a GPS receiver, extra pair of socks, bottle of aspirin, two small flashlights, a hunting knife, small hand towel, whistle, bug spray, sunscreen, snack bars, water, and a roll of toilet paper in a zip lock bag. The toilet paper is good for runny noses, cleaning glasses and for the obvious reason. If you have to use it for the obvious reason be sure to go several yards away from the trail and any water source, dig a hole and cover it up when finished!

We usually keep a pair of slip on water shoes in the car and if it has been raining or we are going to be crossing creeks when the water is running we will throw them in as well. We also take along an extra set of clothes in the car. It is good to have a change of clothes just in case you get wet, muddy, rip something or have been sweating too much and want to change into something that smells better. In the winter we carry a space blanket that you can use to help keep you warm.

TRAIL TYPES

The two trail types described in the book are paved walking trails and the natural hiking trails. The paved trails are mainly walking or biking trails found in the city parks. These trails are fairly level and do not have loose rocks or other obstacles in your way. The natural hiking trails are those trails that take you over the natural terrain of the area. There will be ledges, loose rocks, steep hills, mud, water, creeks, steps, slippery rocks, uneven footing, etc. Each trail is different and requires varying degrees of ability and endurance. That is why we have the trail ratings.

TRAIL RATINGS & GPS

We have rated the trails easy, moderate or difficult. These rating are subjective in that what may be easy for one would be moderate or even difficult for another. In rating the trails we are assuming that the person has been hiking before, is in average physical shape and does not have any major physical problems.

If you are new to hiking and are not use to walking up and down hills over uneven footing or have physical problems you should probably start with one on the paved walking trails. If you have no problems move on to one of the easy natural trails such as the Picnic Trail, Juniper Trail or Chinquapin Trail. Continue to move up to the moderate trails and then the difficult trails as you gain ability and confidence.

The difficult trails are usually a moderate trail with a short section of the trail that is difficult. For those that are in fairly good shape and have been hiking for awhile you should be able to handle a difficult trail if you take your time, stop and rest if you need to and drink plenty of water.

For those with GPS guidance systems the GPS readings under each trail will help you find the trail head a little easier.

CALORIES BURNED

We have included the calories burned for each hiking trail. In determining the number of calories burned there are several factors that must be considered, like how fast you are hiking, your physical condition, your weight, the difficultly of the trail, the temperature, etc. As you can see there is no way to calculate exactly how many calories are burned by each individual person, so these are just good estimates.

To help us in determining the amount of calories burned we used the website of Prevention Magazine at prevention.com. Go to the website, click on the "Weight Loss" heading across the top. Then, scroll down to the "Calorie Burner" along the left edge. In the box, scroll down and click "Walking" and then click "find". This brings up a window where you again select an activity, number of minutes, your weight and click the button "Burn'em". This will give you a general idea of the calories burned for a particular exercise.

When figuring the amount of calories burned for each trail we used two different activities, "hiking cross country" and "3.5 mph brisk" with a person of 170 lbs. For the paved trails and some of the shorter, level natural trails, we used the "3.5 mph brisk" formula. For the other trails we used the "hiking cross country" formula. This gives us a good idea of the amount of calories that we will burn during each hike.

SAFETY ON THE TRAIL

We want everyone's hiking trip to be enjoyable and safe. Several of the trails are close to town where emergency help is not far away. But for some of the trails medical help is not close by and may be difficult to get help to you or get you out. Therefore, we must be as careful and responsible as we can.

Before you leave to go hiking, especially on the natural trails, make sure someone knows where you are going and about what time you will be back. I know, for those of you that are visiting and staying in a motel that may not be convenient. What you can do is leave a note at the front desk or leave one in your room describing what trails you are going to hike and about what time you will be back. That way, if something does happen, there is at least a starting point to begin looking for you.

Take your cell phone along with you. Almost all of the trails in the area will have cell phone reception. There may be some areas where you will lose reception once in awhile but most of the time you will have access to the outside world.

If you do experience problems be sure and call 911. The 911 service is available in all of Branson and most of the surrounding area. Let the dispatcher know what trail you are on, where you are located on the trail and the type of emergency that you have. That is where carrying our book will help. By following the map and trail description you could guide someone to the part of the trail where you are.

For those of you that have children make sure they have a whistle and that they understand a couple of rules.

1. As soon as they realize that they are lost they are to hug a tree. That is, do not walk around, stay put!
2. Use the whistle only in an emergency. When they realize they are lost or hurt, blow the whistle in a series of three so others can hear them and know where they are. A series of three is a signal for help.

Your voice does not carry very well out in the woods, but a whistle can be heard for quite a ways. So make sure the kids have one and know how and when to use it.

CAR REPAIRS

There is nothing like going on a trip and your car breaks down. And it is even worse if you are new to the area. Who do you call? Who can you trust? Well, I have the answer, Art's Auto in downtown Branson. Art and his crew will treat you fairly and get the job done right. If you need Art's help give him a call at 417.334.SERV (7378).

TRAILHEAD DIRECTIONS

All of the directions to the trailheads will begin at the point where highway 76 and highway 65 cross in downtown Branson. We will be going north or south on highway 65 or east or west on highway 76 starting from the **X** on the map. All directions and mileage will be from this point. To help you in getting around while you are in Branson be sure and get a free map of the Branson area at almost any gas station, convince store or restaurant. These maps are provided to the members of the Chamber of Commerce just for the purpose of helping our visitors find their way around town. So don't be bashful about asking for one, it will help tremendously in finding the best route to your destination. Branson has done, and is continuing to do, a great job in the building and maintaining alternate roads around town.

STARTING POINT MAP

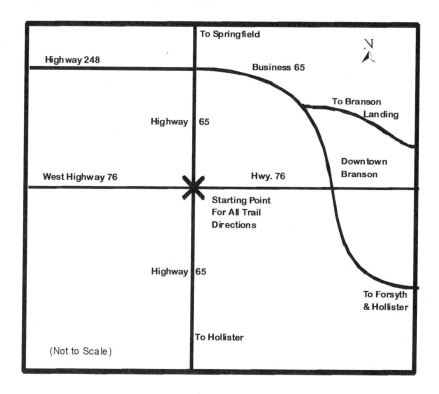

TRAIL DESCRIPTIONS

We have done our best to describe each trail so you will be able to hike the trail and not get lost, along with giving you a good idea of what you can expect to see. We also try to give you landmarks that will help you find your way. There are shortcut trails and side trails that we may not describe so if you decide to hike them you will be on your own.

Even though we have done our best to make sure you do not get lost we can not take any responsibility if you do. There may be a mistake in our description, although we have done our best to check and double check the information. Also, those in charge of maintaining the trails will make new ones or change the layout of an old trail from time to time. If take our book along and pay attention to where the trail is in relation to any major roads, lakes or other land marks and you should not have any problems finding your way around.

In the trail description you will see the letters **SGV** which means it is a spot with a **Super Great View**. We hope you enjoy the view as much as we do.

BRANSON PARKS & RECREATION

Branson has a progressive parks department that is always looking for ways to preserve areas around the community for recreation and enjoyment opportunities for all of its citizens and visitors alike.

The Branson Park Department oversees 13 parks ranging from the small, one acre Epps Park, located at the corner of Long and Adams Street, to the 130 acre wilderness area just off of busy highway 76 on Fall Creek Road. The city parks total more than 265 acres which provide us with many opportunities for hiking, walking, biking, softball, basketball, tennis, golf, skate boarding, soccer, picnicking, bird watching and other activities. Some of the parks have playground equipment for the kids, pavilions for family outings, and even a place to park your RV at the Branson RV Park located on the shores of Lake Taneycomo.

The 42 acre RecPlex is the newest addition to the parks department and opened in 2005. It features a 44,000 square foot recreation center that has two gyms, a fitness center, aerobic and exercise rooms, indoor track, locker rooms, community rooms, game room, concession area and houses the park offices. That is just inside! Outside there is a 12,000 square foot water park which has a zero-depth entry pool area, leisure pool, two water slides, six lap lanes, diving well and shaded picnic area. The AquaPlex is open Monday – Saturday from Memorial Day to Labor Day with a small daily entry fee. There are also four softball fields, soccer fields, pavilions, walking trails and a playground.

We will be describing trails in four different parks in the city of Branson;

Lakeside Forest Wilderness Area
RecPlex
Stockstill Park Walking Trail
Sunset Park Walking Trail

For more information on any of the Branson City Parks you can call 417.335.2368 or visit their website at *bransonparksandrecreation.com.*

LAKESIDE FOREST WILDERNESS AREA

The city of Branson purchased this land in 1998 from Dr. Lyle Owen and is managed by the Branson Parks and Recreation Department. Along with the help of Boy Scout Troops, Eagle Scouts, and volunteers there have been many hours devoted to developing the trails in this area. Consisting of 130 acres it has been designated as a wilderness area to help preserve part of the Ozarks for future generations to see and enjoy.

Dr. Owen purchased this property in 1934 when he was only 27. As a college professor, who taught in schools away from this area, he did not spend much time here until he retired in 1973. His mother lived here for many years while Dr. Owen and his family lived elsewhere.

Dr. Owen and family are the ones that built the stone steps on the Stairway Trail and researched the history of the Gayler family who lived in the cave on the Old Soldiers Cave Trail. Go to our website hikebranson.com for more information on the history of the cave and the stone steps of the Stairway Trail.

In the spring there are several redbud, dogwood trees and different types of flowers that are in bloom. So be sure and bring your camera and binoculars! You may see deer, birds, lizards, squirrels, butterflies, etc. especially, if you hike early morning or in the evening. There is a porta potty at the trailhead. Dogs may be on trail if they are on a leash but may not go down the stairs. Be sure to clean up any messes that your pet makes! There is no camping or fires of any kind in this area. The three trails in this area are;

Old Soldiers Cave Trail
Picnic Trail
Stairway Trail

The Old Soldier's Cave Trail and the Stairway Trail are both rated difficult because of the stairs. The rest of the trail is moderate. When going back up the stairs stop and rest often and it will not be as difficult.

OLD SOLDIER'S CAVE TRAIL   2.8 miles

GPS: N 36' 33.294 W 93' 14.918
Trail Length: 2.8 miles round trip
Trail Type: Natural & Stone Steps
Average Hiking Time: 2 hours
Rating: Difficult (Stairs)
Calories Burned: 920

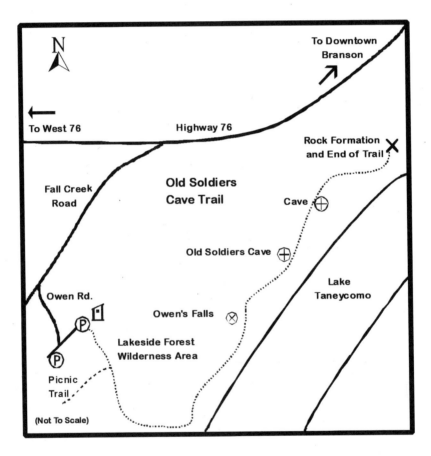

DIRECTIONS TO TRAILHEAD

From the highway 65/76 junction go west on highway 76 for 1.2 miles and turn left onto Fall Creek Road. Go another 0.2 miles and turn left onto Owens Drive at the Lakeside Forest

Wilderness Area sign. Note that the gates are shut at dusk! Drive up the hill and turn left into the upper parking lot and trailhead.

DESCRIPTION OF TRAIL

This trail is not only interesting and of historical significance but is also one of the newest trails in the Branson park system. A lot of work was done in 2005 to open it up so that the hiking public could enjoy the beauty of this lakeside trail. The caves which you will see on your hike were once used by Calvin Gayler to hide himself and his family from the Union forces during the Civil War. The Gayler homestead was originally located in what is now the Branson Landing in downtown Branson. Their home, barn, corrals and other outbuildings were in the area between where the Branson Railroad Station is located and Lake Taneycomo. But in the early years of the war, under orders of General Nathaniel Lyon, Calvin's home and all of his belongings were burned to the ground. He had to find a place to hide and work if he and his family were to survive this terrible war. Remembering this cave, which was located on his property, from one of his previous hunting trips, Calvin moved his wife, Cassandra and their ten children into this cave where they lived for about four years until the end of the war.

The cave, as you will see it today, has a larger opening than it did when the Gayler family lived there in the 1860's but the rest of the cave is much as it was when they survived the frightful years of the Civil War. For more history on the Calvin Gayler family and the Old Soldier's Cave see our website at *hikebranson.com.*

The beginning of the trail to Owens Falls is the same as hiking the Stairway Trail, except we will continue on past the falls. This may not be a good trail for young children. The trail below Owens Falls has loose rocks and can be slippery when they are wet. So proceed with caution. Also, the little ones may have a hard time coming back up the stairs. I know, I had to carry my granddaughter back up the last part of the steps!

If you do have young children, I would take them to the top of the stairs and then take them on the Picnic Trail.

The trailhead is to the right of the porta potty. There is a map of the trails in front of you on a tree stump. It isn't the best map so that is why you have this book! Get your camera, water, binoculars and be sure and use the porta potty, especially if you have children, and let's begin!

The first part of the trail is pretty level and you will see some sign posts that identify different types of trees and plants. If you are lucky enough to be here in early spring you will see a lot of redbud and dogwood trees in bloom and in the fall, lots of color!

Continue straight ahead for about 0.1 miles and you will see a bench on your right. The trail you see to the right of the bench is the beginning of the 1.4 mile Picnic Trail. We will continue to go straight ahead.

At 0.2 miles you will come to another bench and the trail will go slightly down hill. To your left you will begin to see glimpses of Lake Taneycomo and the beautiful valley below.

At 0.3 miles you will come to a wooden overlook. Climb the steps for a SGV. The land you see across the lake is the College of the Ozarks. If you look straight ahead, on top of the hill, you will see a large white building. To the left of the building is the runway for the airport.

On your right, as you leave the overlook, notice all the flowers and the rock wall a few feet above. This is part of the Owens' homestead. After about 30 yards you will be at the stone steps. There is a metal gate with a sign that says, "Do Not Enter". The steps going up lead to the old Owens' house. There are a lot more flowers all around the house, but since the sign says "Do Not Enter" we will turn around and take the steps down toward the lake. There are handrails most of the way down but you still need to take your time and be careful, especially if the steps are wet!

While watching your step, take time to notice the SGV on the way down. There are rocks and stone benches that you can take advantage of on your way down to rest and enjoy the scenery.

At 0.4 miles you will see a small cave on your left. It only goes back about 20 yards and dead ends. But go in and check it out. It is also a cool place to rest when it is hot outside. In wet weather there is a little stream of water that flows out of it.

After the next flight of steps you will come to a rubber mat on the step. Under the mat is an inscription that was put there by the Owens back in 1938. It has faded over the years but what it says is on the plaque attached to the handrail. You may lift the mat and look under it but be sure to put it back. At the next to last step is another mat with another inscription. It is so worn you can't really tell what it says. If you look closely you can make out the name of Owen. Again, be sure and put the mat back in its place before you leave.

This next section of the trail is pretty level and follows along side the bluff just above Lake Taneycomo. During the rainy season it can be muddy and slick so watch your step.

At 0.6 mile you will come to some wooden steps that over-look Owens Falls. There usually isn't any water running unless you happen to be here just after a good rainfall. There may be a sign at the top of the wooden steps that says, "End of Trail". This was true at one time but there has been a lot of work done in extending this part of the trail back up to the trailhead where we started and along the bluff back toward the Old Soldiers Cave. So if the sign is still there just step over the chain and continue on down along the edge of the bluff. There will be some stone steps that will go down to your right that takes you across the bottom of the falls.

Be very careful on this part of the trail. There are loose rocks and if they are wet they will be slick! As you get across the bottom of the falls follow the steps that are along the bluff and head up hill. When you get up on the other side of the falls the trail levels off and you are now at the 0.7 mile point.

Continue following the trail straight ahead as it goes along the edge of the bluff. This is a beautiful hike early in the morning with the sun coming up and the fog rising up off the lake.

At 0.8 miles there is a big leaning tree and just on the other side of it is the Old Soldier's Cave. I hope you brought a flashlight because you will need it if you want to have a good look around. It is a fairly large room that is about 8-9 feet tall in the center and about 30-35 feet across at the widest points. Can you imagine ten to twelve people living in this cave for about four years? It is truly amazing what some people have had to go through in order to survive. I am glad that we are fortunate enough that we have not had to experience living conditions such as this!

After leaving the first cave we will continue back on the trail for about 0.1 mile where we come to another cave. This cave is a tall narrow passage that winds itself back into the hillside for several yards. It is not really big enough to live in but it was probably used by Calvin, along with other caves in the area, to store food and other supplies that they needed for survival during the war.

When you are finished exploring get back on the trail and follow along the bluff line. Notice the water marks on the bluff that have been etched in the rock from the flooding that occurred before the dams were built on the White River. As we approach the 1.1 mile point the trail will narrow and there is a place that often is muddy even in the middle of the summer. We also will go through the "eye of the needle". This is a tree that has grown into an arch over the trail. I am not sure how long this interesting formation will stay around because the tree doesn't seem to be in real good condition, so enjoy it while you can. Oh, by the way, DUCK!

At 1.3 miles there is a SGV of the lake as we go under some power lines way above our heads. The trail narrows again and goes through some cane with a lot of vines growing making it look more like a jungle.

Then we come upon a large, unique rock formation at 1.4 miles. Take a few minutes to rest and explore. But be careful not to cross over onto private property and not to fall off of anything. It would not be easy getting help into this area.

The Branson Parks Department has plans to extend this trail another 0.4 miles and come out at Sunset Park which is located below the highway 65 bridge that crosses Lake Taneycomo. But for now, we will turn around and hike our way back to the trailhead.

When you get back to the stairs be sure and take your time. There are benches along the way where you can stop to rest or just set on the steps if you need to. We are not in a hurry, so take it easy. Soon we are back up at the top. Follow the trail back to the trailhead for a hike of 2.8 miles. Now, if you hiked this everyday you would be in great shape!

> *"Above all, do not lose your desire to walk. Every day I walk myself into a state of well-being and walk away from every illness. I have walked myself into my best thoughts, and I know of no thought so burdensome that one cannot walk away from it."*
> *—Soren Kierkegaard*

> *"The best fitness program in the world are my own two legs."*
> *—Bob Gard*

PICNIC TRAIL

1.4 miles

GPS: N 36'33.294   W 93'14.918
Trail Length: 1.4 miles
Trail Type: Natural
Average Hiking Time: 1 – 1.5 hours
Rating: Easy to Moderate
Calories Burned: 460 – 690

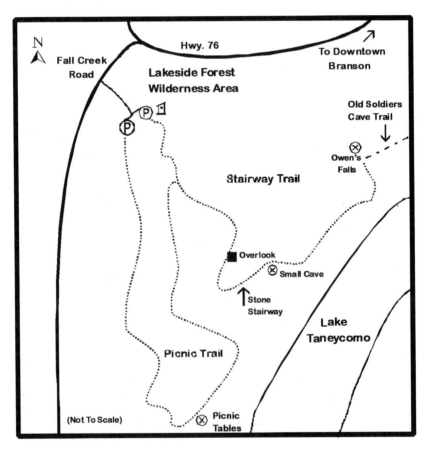

DIRECTIONS TO TRAILHEAD

Follow the same directions as the Old Soldier's Cave Trail.

DESCRIPTION OF TRAIL

The trail begins to the right of the porta potty. Get your camera, binoculars, water, picnic lunch, make sure the kids have used the restroom and let's go!

Follow the woodchip trail out through the woods. Along each side of the trail you will notice some posts that have descriptions of different types of trees and plants. At about 0.1 miles you will see a bench and a trail taking off to your right. The trail straight ahead is the Stairway Trail. We are going to take the trail to the right.

We will soon cross a service road, the old road to the Owens' house, and continue on through the woods. In early spring you will see a lot of dogwood trees in bloom. This is a good trail for a leisurely walk.

At about 0.2 miles look on the right side of the trail for a tree that has a hole in it at ground level. These holes make good places for little creatures to make a home. Just past the tree, on the left, you can see the remains of an old woven wire fence.

Then at about 0.4 miles the trail will curve to the left and start a gradual incline up to the top of the hill. It isn't very steep and it is only a short distance until we reach the top. So, just take your time and enjoy your time outdoors.

Just before we get to the top of the trail we will go over ledge rock. It is pretty easy going and there is even a handrail to help you! Then, before you know it, we are at the top of the hill standing in a cedar glade. There is a bench on your right and usually a woodchip pile on your left that is used to maintain the trail. To the left of the woodchip pile there is a sign that says "Private Property". This is the way to the old Owens' house. At this time they do not want us to go that direction so we will stay on the main trail and go across the top of the hill through the glade.

Notice the bigger cedar trees in this area with their twisted trunks that have weathered many a storm. Even though it is nearly impossible to see, because of all the cedar trees, Lake Taneycomo is below you on your left. Since we can't see the lake be on the lookout for things of interest like, birds, butter-flies, lizards, squirrels, and wild flowers along the trail.

Soon, at 0.7 miles, we come to a couple of picnic tables. Did you remember to bring a lunch? I hope you did! This is good time to relax and enjoy the beauty that is all around us. It is hard to see in the summer time, but when the leaves are off the trees you can look across the lake and see the chapel at the College of the Ozarks. To the right of the chapel is the Hollister water tower. When you get ready to leave be sure and clean up and put any trash in the trash can.

We will continue the trail as it goes slightly downhill and winds out through the woods. At 0.8 miles be looking for a big tree, on your right, that is half alive and half dead. The front half, toward the trail, is alive and the back half is dead. Have you found it, yet? I wonder how much longer this tree is going to last?

On the right side of the trail, at 0.9 miles, we will come to another bench. Sit and rest a spell if you want. The trail now turns to the left and heads downhill and under a power line. At the bottom of the hill we will cross a small wet weather creek that can be a little muddy at times.

When we reach the 1.0 mile point of the trail we come to another tree with a hole at the bottom of it on the back side. This is a little bigger tree than the other one that we saw earlier. After we go past the tree the trail will start a gradual incline as we work our way back up to the parking lot. If you need to take a break there will be a couple more benches coming up on the right side of the trail.

Finally, we come out on the lower level of the parking lot. Turn right and head uphill back to the trailhead. Good job! You just hiked 1.4 miles!

"When you have worn out your shoes, the strength of the shoe leather has passed into the fiber of your body. I measure your health by the number of shoes and hats and clothes you have worn out."
—Ralph Waldo Emerson

STAIRWAY TRAIL

1.2 miles

GPS:	N 36'33.294 W 93'14.918
Trail Length:	1.2 miles
Trail Type:	Natural & Stone Steps
Average Hiking Time:	1 – 1.5 hours
Rating:	Difficult (Stairs)
Calories Burned:	500 – 700

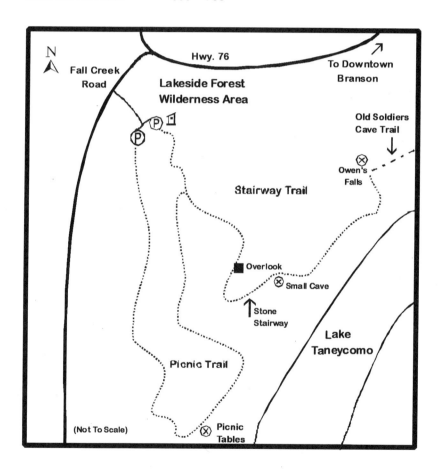

DIRECTIONS TO TRAILHEAD

Follow the same directions as the Old Soldier's Cave Trail.

DESCRIPTION OF TRAIL

The beginning of the trail, to the top of the stairs, is an easy hike. Then the rest is moderate to difficult, mainly because of coming back up the stairs. If you take your time and rest often you should not have any problems. But it is not for young children. If you do have young children I would take them to the top of the stone stairs to enjoy the views and then go back and hike the Picnic Trail.

The trailhead is to the right of the porta potty. There is a map of the trails in front of you on a tree stump. It isn't the best map so that is why you have this book! Get your camera, water, binoculars and be sure and use the porta potty, especially if you have children, and let's begin!

The first part of the trail is pretty level and you will see some sign posts that identify different types of trees and plants. If you are lucky enough to be here in early spring you will see a lot of redbud and dogwood trees in bloom and in the fall, lots of color!

At 0.1 miles you will see a bench on your right. The trail you see to the right of the bench is the beginning of the 1.4 mile Picnic Trail. We will continue to go straight.

At 0.2 miles you will come to another bench and the trail will go slightly down hill. To your left you will begin to see glimpses of Lake Taneycomo and the beautiful valley below.

At 0.3 miles you will come to a wooden overlook. Climb the steps for a SGV. The land you see across the lake is the College of the Ozarks. If you look straight ahead, on top of the hill, you will see a large white building. To the left of the building is the runway for the airport.

On your right, as you leave the overlook, notice all the flowers and the rock wall a few feet above. This is part of the Owens' homestead. After about 30 yards you will be at the stone steps. There is a metal gate with a sign that says, "Do Not Enter". The steps going up lead to the old Owens' house. There are a lot more flowers all around the house, but since the sign says "Do Not Enter" we will turn around and take the steps down toward the lake. There are handrails most of the way down but you still need to take your time and be careful, especially if the steps are wet!

While watching your step, take time to notice the SGV on the way down. There are rocks and stone benches that you can take advantage of on your way down to rest and enjoy the scenery.

At 0.4 miles you will see a small cave on your left. It only goes back about 20 yards and dead ends. But go in and check it out. It is also a cool place to rest when it is hot outside. In wet weather there is a little stream of water that flows out of it.

After the next flight of steps you will come to a rubber mat on the step. Under the mat is an inscription that was put there by the Owens back in 1938. It has faded over the years but what it says is on the plaque attached to the handrail. You may lift the mat and look under it but be sure to put it back. At the next to last step is another mat with another inscription. It is so worn you can't really tell what it says. If you look closely you can make out the name of Owen. Again, be sure and put the mat back in its place before you leave.

This next section of the trail is pretty level and follows along side the bluff just above Lake Taneycomo. During the rainy season it can be muddy and slick so watch your step.

At 0.6 mile you will come to some wooden steps that overlook Owens Falls. There usually isn't any water running unless you happen to be here just after a good rainfall.

This is the end of the Stairway Trail but if you want to you can go on down below the falls but just be very careful of loose, wet rocks. There is a trail that goes on across the bottom of the falls and goes to the Old Soldiers Cave. If you want to continue follow the trail description under the Old Soldiers Cave Trail.

For the rest of us we will turn around and hike back up to the trailhead. Remember to take your time going back up the steps. They are the hardest part of the trail so rest often. After getting back up to the top of the stairs enjoy the view from the overlook one more time before heading back to your car.

"Me thinks that the moment my legs begin to move, my thoughts begin to flow."
—Henry David Thoreau

RECPLEX WALKING TRAILS

GPS:	N 36' 42.254 W 93' 14.406
Trail Length:	Different Lengths, 0.5 and more
Trail Type:	Paved
Rating:	Easy
Calories Burned:	155 for each 30 minutes walked

The 42 acre RecPlex is the newest addition to the parks department and opened in 2005. It features a 44,000 square foot recreation center that has two gyms, a fitness center, aerobic and exercise rooms, indoor walking track, locker rooms, community rooms, game room, concession area and also houses the park offices. This is just inside! Outside there is a 12,000 square foot water park which has a zero-depth entry pool area. The AquaPlex is open Monday – Saturday from Memorial Day to Labor Day with a small daily entry fee. There are also four softball fields, soccer fields, pavilions, walking trails and a playground.

There are several paved paths around the park. One loop takes you around the recreation center and water park. There is also a loop that takes you all the way around the outside edge of the park with several cross connecting paths that allows you to walk a different way each time around. There are also paths that will take you up to highway 248 or down to highway 65.

There are signs that show the different walking trails and the mileage for each one. To get more information on the hours, fees, availability of pavilions, etc. give the Branson City Park a call at 417.335.2368.

DIRECTIONS TO RECPLEX

From highway 76/65 go north on highway 65 to the Bee Creek/Branson Hills Pkwy. Exit at 1.5 miles. Turn left and go about 1.8 miles and you will see the RecPlex on your left.

Description of Trail

Indoors: For those days that are not so nice you can always go inside to get your exercise. Inside the Recreation Center there is a walking path that goes around the basketball courts. Twelve laps = one mile.

Outdoors: As we stated earlier, there are several paths that go around and cross the Park. There are information signs pointing out the different trails and their mileage.

You can also do some walking outside of the park along the Branson Hills Parkway that will take you up to highway 248 or down to the Target and Home Depot Stores by highway 65.

If you walk out of the Recreation Center and go to your left, follow the path that goes along the Parkway and it will take you 0.7 miles to highway 248. So the walk up to the highway and back will be 1.4 miles.

If you go to the right upon leaving the Recreation Center and follow the path along the Parkway you can walk 1.5 miles down to the Target and Home Depot Stores. If you walk on down another 0.3 miles you will come to the welcome center at the gas station. There is a pedestrian cross walk that you will need to use at 1.1 miles to get you to the other side of the Parkway which is where the stores are located.

So if you walk to the Target Store and back it is 3.0 miles. To the Welcome Center and back will be 3.6 miles. That is not counting any walking you do in the stores.

"Our way is not soft grass, it's a mountain path with lots of rocks. But it goes upward, forward, toward the sun."

Ruth Westheimer

STOCKSTILL PARK WALKING TRAIL

0.5 miles

GPS:	N 36′ 38.900 W 93′ 14.296
Trail Length:	0.5 miles
Trail Type:	Paved
Average Hiking Time:	15 minutes per lap
Rating:	Easy
Calories Burned:	80 per lap

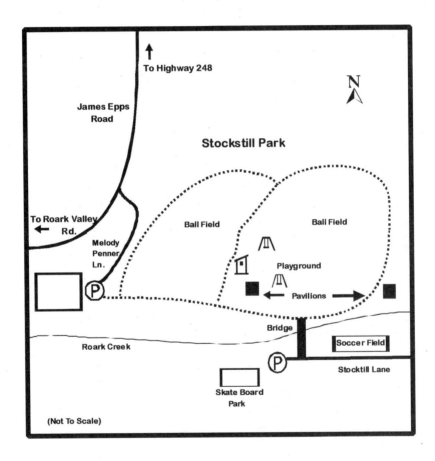

This is a popular park, especially with families. There is something for everyone with two ball fields, walking track, pavilion, and playground equipment for kids of all ages, a skate board park, soccer field, tennis courts, and a creek.

In the summer during game time there is a concession stand. And yes, there are restrooms and a drinking fountain.

DIRECTIONS TO TRAILHEAD

There are two ways into this park. The description of the trail is given from the East entrance parking lot. If you come in from the West Entrance just park your car and begin the trail to your left as you enter the park and follow the description of the trail where it mentions the West parking lot.

EAST ENTRANCE

From highway 65 take highway 76 West through the first stop light. Get in the right lane and two blocks from the stop light turn right on Walnut Lane. There is a brown information sign that points the way to the park. Go one block to a stop sign then one more block and turn left onto Stockstill Lane. There is another brown information sign the points the way. Follow the road down the hill to the railroad tracks. Be sure and look both ways because this is an active track. The park begins just on the other side of the tracks.

There will be a soccer field on your right, a skate board park on the left and a parking lot in the middle. There is a wooden foot bridge that takes you across Roark Creek to the trail and the rest of the park.

WEST ENTRANCE

You can reach the West entrance of the park from Roark Valley Road or Highway 248. We will begin with Roark Valley Road. From highway 65 go West on highway 76. Get in the right lane and it will merge into Roark Valley Road at the stop light. Take Roark Valley Road down the hill to the next stop light. Turn right onto James F. Epps road, cross over bridge and you will see tennis courts and the park on your right. Turn right on Melody Penner Lane to parking lot.

You can also go north on highway 65 from the 76/65 junction for about 0.7 miles and take the highway 248 exit. At the stop light turn left onto highway 248, go about one mile to another stop light. There will be a McDonalds across the intersection on your left. Turn left on James F. Epps road. There is a school up ahead so if you see a yellow flashing signal do not go over 30 miles an hour. Go about a mile to bottom of the hill and turn left onto Melody Penner road.

DESCRIPTION OF TRAIL

The trail is laid out in a figure eight pattern around the two ball fields. The trail begins on the other side of the bridge from the parking lot. We will start our walk by going to your right.

The ball field to your left is Huff field. At the end of the field there will be a pavilion on your right. Go on around the ball field, past the swings where you will turn left between the play ground equipment and the second ball field named Kiewitt.

You will see the restrooms on your left then the trail will continue to your right around Kiewitt field. Roark Creek will be on your left.

At the end of the field you will see the parking lot for the West entrance to the park. Follow the trail on around the field and soon you will go past Old Glory on your left.

Turn right and go between the play ground and Kiewitt field past the restrooms and this time take the trail to your left as you go past the play ground on your left and the creek on your right. When you come to the bridge you have completed one lap and 0.5 miles

SUNSET PARK WALKING TRAIL   0.6 miles

GPS: N 36' 38.257   W 93' 13.572
Trail Length: 0.6 miles per lap
Trail Type: Paved
Average Walking Time: 15 minutes per lap
Rating: Easy
Calories Burned: 90 per lap

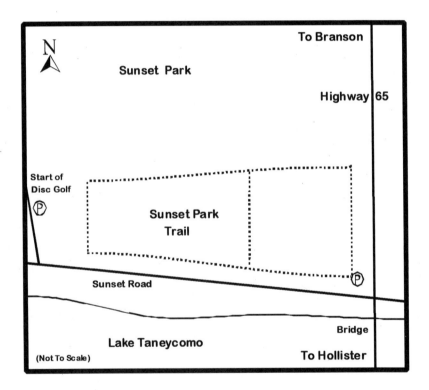

SUNSET PARK WALKING TRAIL/DISC GOLF COURSE

This beautiful little park is located right next to Lake Taneycomo. It is a popular walking trail with the locals because it usually isn't crowded and being next to the lake it is a little cooler on those hot summer evenings. This park is open from 6am till 11pm and has lights so you can even walk after it gets dark. Dogs can be on the trail but only on a leash. All dog owners are asked to please clean up after their pets! There are really three parks in this area. The first park you will come to is Joe C. Alexander Park. It has two ball fields, a tennis court, a small playground and restrooms. After you go under the highway 65 bridge you come to Sunset Park and within this park is a Disc (Frisbee) Golf Course. We will discuss the course later.

DIRECTIONS TO TRAILHEAD

From the highway 76/65 junction, go east on highway 76 toward the downtown area. As you go down the hill get in the right hand lane. At the stoplight at the bottom of the hill take a right onto Business 65. Go about 0.4 miles and turn right on Hensley St. Just before you turn you will see a brown information sign on your right that says "Alexander Park". You will be going right past this park so follow the signs. (If you go across the Taneycomo bridge you have gone too far!) Stay on Hensley until you come to the second stop sign then turn left on Fifth St. There you will see another brown direction sign. Turn left and go to the stop sign at the bottom of the hill and turn left onto Hawthorne St. Here you will see Alexander Park on your right. Follow the road on around the park, go under the highway 65 bridge and the trailhead and parking are on your right. If you want to play Disc Golf go on down about 0.2 miles to the parking area at the other end of the park.

DESCRIPTION OF TRAIL

The trail is laid out in a figure eight. We will begin by taking the path to the right. As you walk around the trail there are white arrows on the trail that point you in the direction you are suppose to walk. Just a word of caution, there is a lot of poison ivy just off the trail that goes along side the highway and the bluff. So make sure that you and the kids stay in the mowed area of the park.

DISC GOLF COURSE

For something a little different you might try your skill at Disc Golf. It is fun but it is harder than it looks, at least for me. On the far end (West end) of Sunset Park is a parking lot and the beginning of the Disc Golf Course. There you will find a list of the rules. The course is 2706 feet long and a par 27. The object of the game is to throw the Disc and get it into a metal cup attached to a pole. There are metal chains hanging just above the cup. By throwing the Disc into the chains the Disc stops and falls into the cup. I just used a Frisbee but it is a little harder to get into the cup because of it's lighter weight. They tell me there is a Disc made just for Golf. I think they are a little smaller, heavier and have a sharper edge to them. If you have children this is something they can do while you are walking. Or better yet, join them!

> *Above all, do not lose your desire to walk. Every day I walk myself into a state of well-being and walk away from every illness. I have walked myself into my best thoughts, and I know of no thought so burdensome that one cannot walk away from it.*
> *Soren Kierkegaard*

MISSOURI DEPARTMENT OF CONSERVATION

The Missouri Department of Conservation was established in 1936 when the citizens of Missouri overwhelmingly passed a constitutional amendment to establish a commission to restore Missouri's wildlife and forests.

In 1976 the citizens of Missouri once again showed their commitment to conservation when they passed another amendment to the constitution establishing a one-eighth of a cent conservation sales tax.

Today, Missouri spends more per capita on conservation than its eight neighboring states and has the third largest conservation budget of the nation.

Missouri is looked up to by other agencies in there operations and management of natural resources. Because of Missourian's commitment to conservation we have many opportunities to enjoy the great outdoors, for today and for many generations to come.

In this section we will be describing eleven trails in five different Missouri Department of Conservation areas. The five conservation areas are:

Boston Ferry Conservation Area
Busiek State Forest & Wildlife Area
Drury - Mincy Conservation Area
Empire District Electric Company Park (Ozark Beach Recreation Area)
Ruth and Paul Henning Forest Conservation Area
Shepherd of the Hills Fish Hatchery

"In every walk with nature one receives more than he seeks."

John Muir

BOSTON FERRY CONSERVATION AREA   1.2 miles

GPS:	N 36' 41.772 W 93' 12.066
Trail Length:	1.2 miles round trip
Trail Type:	Natural
Average Hiking Time:	1 hour
Rating:	Moderate
Calories	Burned: 460

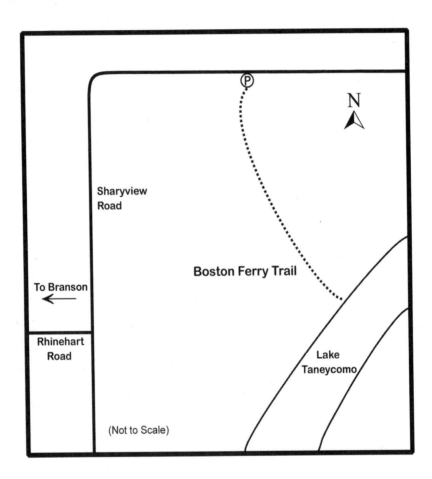

BOSTON FERRY ROAD TRAIL

This land was purchased by William S. Boston in 1870 and a short time later he opened up the Boston Ferry to compete with the Hensley Ferry that was located just down stream on the old White River. These ferries helped to move people, horses and wagons along the Harrison-Springfield road which was the only north-south route in the area from Missouri to Arkansas. It was estimated that fifty to one hundred wagons traveled the road each day.

Today, this part of the land is owned by the Missouri Department of Conservation.

This trail is a little different in that you end up right on the shore of Lake Taneycomo. It is a fairly easy trail to hike. The only problem is that it is down hill all the way from the trailhead to the lake then you have to hike back up. It is not too steep and is easily hiked if you just take your time. The sign says it is 0.5 miles in length. But if you go on down to the lake it is another 0.1 miles which brings the distance to 1.2 miles for the round trip. It is a little brushy the last 0.1 mile so be sure and use some bug spray.

DIRECTIONS TO TRAILHEAD

From highway 76/65 go north on highway 65 for 1.5 miles and take the Bee Creek Road exit. Turn right onto Bee Creek Road. Follow it across a small bridge, up the hill and at 3.4 miles turn right onto Rhinehart Road. Then at 4.1 miles the road turns left at the "T" intersection and becomes Shary View Road. (The house on your left, on the corner, is the house that Janet's dad built and where she grew up). As you approach the 5.0 mile point you will see a parking lot and trailhead on your right.

DESCRIPTION OF TRAIL

Begin to the left of the sign that says, "Boston Ferry Road Trail". Take the trail as it heads downhill toward the lake. You will see some interesting ledge rock along the way that appears to have wagon ruts worn in it.

As we get to the bottom, at 0.4 miles, there will be some large sycamore and walnut trees along the trail as we cross a wet weather creek.

Then at 0.5 miles we reach the end of the trail. Be very quiet and if we are lucky we might get to see some ducks, cranes or other wildlife in the slough or along the shore of the lake. Janet and I got to see a mother duck and her little ducklings swimming around the lake when we were here one spring day.

To your right, at the end of the trail, is a little trail that goes to a slough. Here you will see a large bird house and we are not sure what type of bird it was built for.

Back out on the main trail go down into the wet weather creek bed and follow it out to the lake. Remember, be quiet and you might get to see some wild life. This is a SGV of the lake.

On your way back out notice the large cottonwood trees. They have been here a long time. Now, follow the trail back up the hill for a hike of 1.2 miles.

BUSIEK STATE FOREST

The Busiek State Forest and Wildlife Area is located about 15 miles north of Branson and 18 miles south of Springfield, in Christian county. It is a popular place with the locals for hunting, hiking, horseback riding, bicycling, exploring, target shooting and just enjoying the great outdoors.

The original tract of land was purchased by the Missouri Department of Conservation in 1981 with the help of Dr. Paul Busiek. Since then other tracts have been purchased bringing it to its present size of 2,502 acres.

The two main creeks that flow across this area are the Woods Fork Creek and Camp Creek. You can see places where there were likely homes at one time. The structures are no longer there, at least that we have seen, but you can see where an area had been cleared and plants growing that are usually found around a house. And on the ridge above the Woods Fork and Camp Creek you will see the Carter family cemetery. The cemetery is located on the section of the trail where the red and yellow trails run together.

In hiking the trails you will cross the creeks several times. Most of the time this is no problem but just after a hard rain you may have to be careful where you cross. You might want to bring another pair of shoes to change into, or if you have tough feet, you can just take off your socks and shoes and walk across the creek barefoot. After periods of hard rain the creeks will have a lot of water. Even up into the summer you can usually find enough water to cool your feet, but be aware that parts of the trail will be muddy after it rains.

If you hear gunshots while you are hiking don't be alarmed because there is a public shooting range that is located to the west of the highway 65 bridge. So if you have a gun that needs to be sighted in or you just enjoy shooting, bring it along.

Busiek is usually a pretty busy place on the weekends, especially with horse back riders. If you enjoy a little more peace and quiet for your hikes you may want to go during the week and/or early in the mornings. Or you might want to try the trails located on the west side of highway 65 by going under the bridge. These trails do not seem to be used by horse back riders as much those on the east side.

There are six individual trails in the park. Three are on the east side of highway 65 and three and on the west side, under, highway 65. One trail, the Silver Trail, is more easily accessed by entering from highway "A" off of highway 65. Detailed directions are given under the Silver Trail description. The trails will often overlap and you will be hiking sections of the same trail for each individual trail. This lends itself to hiking sections of two or three trails for a longer hike.

In 2000 and 2001, the boy scouts took on the project of putting up trail markers and color code the main trails. Even with the work done by the boy scouts and the map that is provided by the Conservation Department it is still easy to get turned around. The main trails are marked pretty well, but it is the trail intersections that are not very well marked and are a bit confusing at times. We know, the first time Janet and I hiked this area we got turned around, but after we got back to a section of the trail where we had already hiked we could tell where we made our mistake and got back on trail. If you will follow the directions in the book you should not have any problems. Since there are so many little paths that take off here and there we will describe the main trails and some of the lesser trails. But if you see a side trail that looks interesting, feel free to check it out. You can always turn around and go back.

There are some camping sites, mainly along the creek on the east side of the park. But if you would like to do some camping you will need to get a special use permit. You can do this by writing to: Missouri Department of Conservation, 2630 N. Mayfair, Springfield, Mo. 65803. Or you might want to give them a call, their phone number is 417-895-6880. You can also use this number to report any problems in the park. Janet and I started to hike the Orange Trail one morning and there was a large sycamore tree that had fallen across the entrance to the parking lot. We gave them a call and by the time we had finished our hike they had it all cleaned up!

All six trails have a rating of moderate to difficult but don't let that scare you. The reason we have rated them this way is because each trail has a hill that you must hike up, but if you have been hiking and are in fairly good shape it should not be a problem. The steeper part of the incline usually is no longer than 0.2 miles in length. So when you are going uphill just go slow, take your time and before you know it you are at the top. In our estimation, the easiest trail in the park is the Orange Trail followed by the Purple, White, Red, Yellow and Silver Trail.

If you would like to hike or bike a real easy trail, take the Orange Trail for 2.1 miles until you come to where the trail turns to the right and starts uphill. At this point just turn around and follow the trail back to your car for an easy hike of 4.2 miles. This is a fairly level hike through the Ozark valley where you will cross the creek several times, so if the creek is running you will get your feet wet.

One last note, the mileage listed on the signs and brochures is not exactly what we have come up with. I believe the mileage they show is calculated from where that trail starts as it leaves another trail and not always from the trailhead. The mileage we have listed is the distance from the trailhead at the parking lot and back to the same trailhead.

Each trail can be hiked individually or combined with other trails for a longer hike. So pick out a trail that you would like to hike and let's get going!

BUSIEK RED TRAIL

4.2 miles

GPS:	N 36' 51.722 W 93' 13.533
Trail Length:	4.2 mile loop
Trail Type:	Natural
Average Hiking Time:	3.5 to 4 hours
Rating:	Moderate
Calories Burned:	1,610 – 1,840

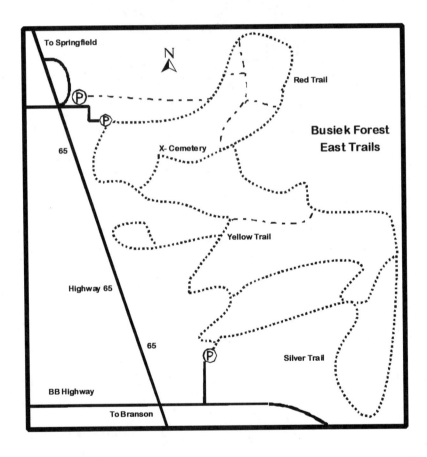

RED TRAIL

DIRECTIONS TO TRAILHEAD

From highway 76 go north on highway 65 for 15.4 miles. You will see a brown information signs on the side of the road directing you to the Busiek area. Turn right onto Busiek Road and follow it ondown the hill. At the bottom of the hill we will turn left, past the first parking lot on the left. This is where most of the horse riders park their trailers. Continue on for a short distance to the second parking lot at the end of the road. The trailhead begins at the back of the parking lot at the information sign behind the metal post.

DESCRIPTION OF TRAIL

If you are standing and facing the information sign which shows the layout of the trails, you will begin by going to your right. Follow the trail through the field. In the summer it is usually mowed. There are camp sites on the right and a creek runs along the back of the campsites. There are some lesser trails that take off from the main trail that leads down to the creek. Go and explore if you want to but just come back to the main trail when you are finished.

At 0.4 miles we join another trail that comes in from our left. This trail is mainly used by the horse back riders that come in from the first parking lot we passed on our way in. We want to take the trail to the right.

Then at 0.5 miles the trail splits. To the right are more camp sites and a shortcut that crosses the creek. We will take the trail to the left as it goes into the woods. On our left, up the side of the hill, we can see where the Conservation Department is doing some restoration work on the glade.

The trail now opens up a little and at 0.6 miles we are at our first creek crossing. Depending on how much water is flowing, and what time of the year it is, you may want that extra pair of shoes I mentioned earlier, or you may just want to enjoy the cool, clear water on your bare feet. The trail resumes on the other side of the creek just to the right of the crooked sycamore tree limb.

After we cross the creek we see where the trail splits again.

The trail to the right is part of the shortcut trail that follows back down along the creek where you can take a right turn and go back across the creek (about 0.1 miles) and then turn back left to the trailhead or continue on along the creek and keep to the right at the other trail junctions and you will connect with the yellow trail just above the Carter cemetery. Stay to your right past the cemetery and back to the trailhead. **But we want to stay on the main Red trail so we will turn left and follow the trail into an open field.**

The trail runs along the edge of the field and then turns to the right as we circle around the back of the field. The trail will then turn to the left as we head up hill through the woods.

As we approach the 1.0 mile point the trail becomes a little steeper. There are some little stumps and loose rocks in this section of the trail so be sure and pick up your feet. The going does get a little rough but just take your time and soon we will be at the top of the hill at 1.2 miles.

Now, the trail turns to the right and we get to go downhill for awhile. There is a lesser trail that takes off from the main trail but the Conservation Department doesn't want us to use it. So we will stay on the main trail.

Not too far down the hill, on our right, is a big oak tree that is leaning out over the hillside. The trail levels out and winds around the side of the hill.

At 0.3 miles the trail turns to the right as we cross a small wet weather creek. A little ways on our left is a ledge rock that is covered in moss. In the summer be sure and notice the little ferns that are growing right out of the rock

As we come to the 1.5 mile point in our hike the trail spits again. The trail to the left is not a hiking trail so we will take the trail to our right as we head downhill. Be looking to your right for a break in the trees where you can see the hills on the other side of the creek that we crossed earlier.

The trail continues to go downhill but now it is a little steeper as we go over some ledge rock. Watch your step. There is a small glade on our left about half way down.

One time while hiking this trail Janet and I encountered a young man riding his bike, and at times carrying his bike, up this hill. In fact he passed us about four times as we hiked the Red trail. Now, we like to ride our bikes but when we think of places to ride this trail isn't one that comes to mind!

At the bottom of the hill, at 1.7 miles, we come to a creek and the trail splits to the left and right. The trail to the right connects to the shortcut trail that we mentioned earlier. We will continue on the main trail so we will take the trail to the left.

After crossing the wet weather creek the trail will once again head uphill. It is a little steep at first but it soon levels off a bit and is not too bad the rest of the way up the hill.

At 1.9 miles the Red trail intersects with the Yellow trail and there is a sign post showing the layout of the trails. There is a lesser trail that is marked as a no hiking trail. The trail to the left is the Yellow trail and the trail to our right is where the Red trail and Yellow trail run together. We want to take the trail to the right.

The trail goes downhill slightly and at 2.0 miles we see, on our right, where the shortcut trail joins back with the main trail.

There are some small glades along the trail that have several different types of wildflowers and ferns. The trail now goes slightly uphill as we go back into the woods.

At 2.3 miles there is a lesser trail that takes off to our right and goes a short distance to an old pond. The water is a little dirty but you can sometimes you can see some birds and other wildlife.

On one of our hikes, Janet and I had just gone past the pond when I heard something in the leaves, to my left, just off the trail. I soon noticed that it was a snake. Now, I like snakes and have had a few as pets. I assumed that it would just take off and go out through the woods. Wrong! Instead it circled on around behind me and came out on the trail right where Janet was. There they were face to face. The yellow racer got up in a defensive striking pose and was ready to bite her if she came any closer. At the same time Janet did some kind of fancy two-step and was standing beside me in a flash! The snake, seeing the coast was clear, went on across the trail and away from us.

I am thankful to say that Janet, nor the snake, were injured in this encounter!

For those of you, who are afraid of snakes, just remember that they will try to avoid you at all cost. If you do see one, try to be calm and ease away slowly. Just to let you know, we have hiked a lot in the past few years and we very seldom see a snake while on the trails. If we do it is usually quite a ways off and trying to get away from us.

Next, at 2.4 miles we will see the Carter cemetery on our right. There are a lot of headstones that date back to the 1800's. Take a little time to look around if you want.

After leaving the cemetery follow the trail on down the hill. At the bottom of the hill we will intersect with the Yellow trail. We will go to the right as we go back to the trailhead.

During the summer you can see some wild roses and black-berries along the trail as we go on down the hill back to the trailhead. There will be some lesser trails that take off to the left as we get closer to the creek. Continue straight ahead along the creek until the trail comes to the creek. You will now need to cross over to the other side to the parking lot.

BUSIEK YELLOW TRAIL

4.3 miles

GPS:	N 36' 51.722 W 93' 13.533
Trail Length:	4.3 miles
Trail Type:	Natural
Average Hiking Time:	3.5 – 4 hours
Rating:	Moderate
Calories Burned:	1,610 – 1,840

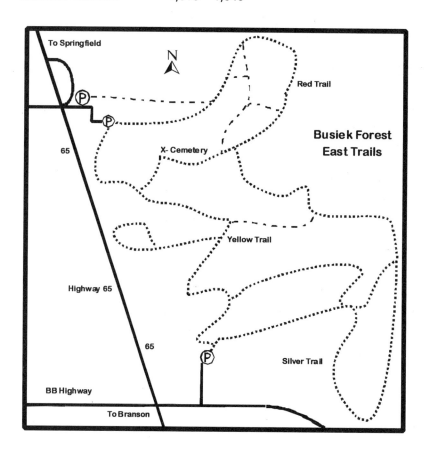

YELLOW TRAIL

DIRECTIONS TO TRAILHEAD

Follow the same directions as those given for the Red Trail.

DESCRIPTION OF TRAIL

If you are facing the information sign the trail will start directly behind you. Turn around and the first thing we will do is go across the creek. If the water is running you can change shoes, go across barefoot or just get your feet wet! After you have made it across the trail will turn to the right as we follow along the creek. We begin our hike in the shade but before you know it the trail opens up into a field and begins to go slightly uphill. There are some blackberry and raspberry patches along the way but there is also a lot of poison ivy! So be very careful, especially if you can't identify it. Remember, leaves of three let it be!

As we approach the 0.3 mile point the trail will split. The trail to the left is the way we will be coming back so we want to continue going straight ahead out through the field.

As we hike out through the field be sure and remain on the trail because there are large poison ivy patches on both sides of the trail. This is the largest patch of poison ivy we have ever seen.

At 0.5 miles you will see a lesser trail that take off to the left. This is not the main trail so we want to go to the right. And then at 0.7 miles we will cross Woods Fork Creek. Most of the time, if it hasn't rained too hard and washed it away, you will get to see the beginnings of a beaver dam.

Right after we cross the creek take the trail to the left as it goes out through an open field. As we enter the field be sure and look around for any wildlife that might be there. Sometimes, if you are lucky, you might get to see deer, turkey, coyotes or other animals that roam the area. As we approach 0.8 miles the trail comes to a "T". To the left is one of the shortcut trails that will come out at the pawpaw patch that we will come to later in our hike. We will go to the right and stay on the main Yellow Trail.

Just as we enter the woods, at 0.9 miles, you can see a trail that takes off to the right. This is what I call the Loop Trail because it loops around the top of a tall hill and comes back down. The trail to the top is fairly steep but has some SGV once you are at the top, especially when the leaves are off. The total distance for the Loop Trail is 1.1 miles. **If you want to hike the Loop Trail you can find the trail description at the end of the Yellow Trail description.**

For those who do not want to hike the Loop Trail or if you hiked the Loop Trail and are ready to continue on with the Yellow Trail, let's go!

This part of the trail is a steady incline with lots of loose rocks, but we soon come out into a small open field once we reach the top. Here you can see some walnut trees and yucca plants that may be an indication of an old homestead.

The trail will now go downhill and then back up as we cross a wet weather creek and yes, it gets steep again. But at 1.3 miles the trail opens up into a glade at the top of the hill. From here there are some SGV of the Ozark hills. The trail to the right is the Silver Trail and leads back to the trailhead on highway A. The trail to the left is the way we want to go and we will be following both the Yellow and Silver Trail for awhile.

On both sides of the trail you will see a cactus patch and throughout the spring and summer they will have some beautiful yellow flowers. After going through the cactus the trail goes uphill slightly and then levels off as we go across the top of the ridge. Janet and I saw three does grazing along this ridge on one of our hikes so be quiet and look out ahead of you and you might get to see a deer or two.

After we get to the other side of the ridge the trail will now go steeply down the side of the hill. Be careful because there are loose rocks and some small trunks of cedar trees placed across the trail to help with erosion. So watch your step and take your time. After reaching the bottom, at 1.9 miles, the trail will level off for a while and then turn back to the left as we cross another small creek. We now go back up hill for a short distance before we come to a trail intersection at 2.1 miles.

To the right is the Silver Trail. We will go to the left and there will be another split in the trail about fifty yards ahead. Again, the trail to the right is part of the Silver Trail so we want to continue on the trail as it goes straight ahead and slightly downhill. The trail will be level for awhile before we come to a clearing at 2.3 miles. This is where the Silver Trail and Yellow Trail part ways, Silver Trail to the right and the Yellow Trail to the left. As we follow the Yellow Trail to the left, we will see some blue tipped post on our right. This marks the boundary between public and private land so make sure to stay on this side of the fence.

At 2.4 miles we will be crossing Woods Fork Creek once again. Soon, after crossing the creek the trail opens up, turns to the left and goes under a power line right of way. After leaving the power lines we have a nice hike through a small field and then back into the woods.

When we get to the 2.9 mile point of our hike, we come to another junction in the trail. We will take the trail to the left, continue ahead for about ten yards and then take the trail that goes to the right, up hill through the woods. The trail that goes straight ahead is a shortcut trail that connects back with the Yellow Trail. This little jog in the trail is also a Pawpaw patch. Pawpaw trees are small and have wide, long leaves. In late summer you can see the light green colored paw paws that are about the size of an apple and are oblong in shape, growing on the trees. The fruit usually ripens in late September, has a light yellow color and is described as tasting like anything from bananas to sweet cantaloupe. If you are here in the fall you might try one and see what it tastes like to you.

The trail will go uphill for a short distance and then level off as we follow along a creek, then cross the creek before we gradually head uphill again. At 3.3 miles the trail opens up along side the hill into a glade with some SGV of the Ozark hills to our south.

As we get to the other side of the glade at 3.4 miles we intersect with the Red Trail. The Red Trail goes to the right but we will follow the Yellow trail that goes to the left. The trail will level off as we go through some glades and back out into the woods. The trail that you see on your right is one of the shortcut trails found on the Red Trail.

At 3.7 miles you will notice a small pond off to your right and at 3.8 miles, we come to the Carter Cemetery. If you want, take some time to look around. There are several flowers growing in and around the cemetery. One of them is the yucca plant which has long, pointed leaves with a tall stalk in the middle and white bell shaped flowers.

When you are ready follow the trail on down the hill. This part of the trail use to go straight down the hill but in 2005 the conservation department rerouted it into a switch back which makes the trail a little longer but easier to hike.

When we reach the bottom of the hill at 4.1 miles we connect back with the main Yellow Trail where we were earlier in our hike. Take the trail to the right and follow it back to the trailhead at 4.3 miles.

LOOP TRAIL DESCRIPTION

The Loop Trail begins by going across a wet weather creek and then comes to a "T" on the other side. We will go to the left. Be sure and **take note of this intersection** because on our way back we want to make sure we go back the same way we came. The trail goes steadily uphill, levels off for a short distance and then back uphill again. If you look close you will see a trail off to the right, this is the way we will be coming back.

At 0.3 miles the trail will split, we want to take the trail to the right. We will still be going uphill but not as steep and then, at 0.5 miles, we finally reach the top! There some SGV, especially if you are here after the leaves are off. Down below you can see highway 65.

We will now head steeply back down the hill over some loose rocks so watch your step. The trail now levels off and becomes pretty brushy. At 0.9 miles we have circled around the hill and have joined back with the Loop Trail. Take the trail downhill to the left and at 1.0 miles we are back at the first trail intersection we came to earlier. **Make sure you go to the right!** We will cross the creek and at 1.1 miles we are back to the Yellow Trail. Take the trail to the right and continue to follow the description of the Yellow Trail. Make sure you add 1.1 miles to the 4.3 miles of the Yellow Trail for a total hiking distance of 5.4 miles.

BUSIEK SILVER TRAIL

3.1 miles

GPS: N 36' 50.556   W 93' 12.765
Trail Length: 3.1 mile loop
Trail Type: Natural
Average Hiking Time: 2.5 to 3 hours
Rating: Difficult
Calories Burned: 1,150 – 1,380

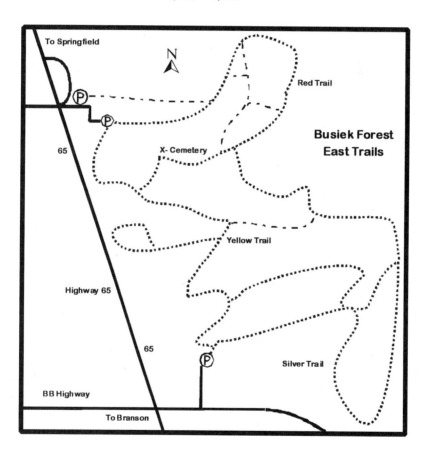

SILVER TRAIL

DIRECTIONS TO TRAILHEAD

From highway 76 go north on highway 65 for 13.8 miles and turn right onto state highway A. Go 0.2 miles and turn left onto a gravel service road. At the entrance to the road there should be a yellow conservation sign and it will look as though you are turning in the driveway of the house that is on your left. After going 0.2 miles down the gravel road you will come to a large parking lot. The trailhead is behind the cabled post on the left as you enter the parking lot.

DESCRIPTION OF TRAIL

Most of this trail is what we would call moderate but there is one hill that is difficult. For about 0.2 miles you will be hiking up a pretty steep hill. If you are in good shape and have been doing some hiking you can make it, Janet and I have several times.

We begin by starting to the right of the information sign and following an old road downhill. At 0.1 mile we want to take the trail that goes to our left. The first time Janet and I hiked this trail we took the trail straight ahead and hiked in a counter clockwise direction. Mistake! We had climb two steep hills! By going to our left we will only have one steep hill to climb. As you will see, that will be enough! As we continue, the trail follows along side a wet weather creek then turns to the right, crosses the creek and heads gradually uphill.

After a little incline the trail levels off for a nice hike through the woods. At 0.3 miles we come out of the woods into a clearing and we intersect with the yellow trail. The trail to the left is the yellow trail. Note: there is a lesser trail further to our left that goes up hill. This is not a hiking trail so we will take the trail to our right. The yellow and silver trail will run together for awhile.

In the small glade right in front of us, notice the cactus growing on both sides of the trail. If you are here during late spring and summer you will get to see a lot of beautiful yellow blossoms.

Right after the cactus plants the trail will go slightly up hill across the top of the ridge. There certainly isn't any shade to be found here! So enjoy the view of the hills all around us. The ridge was cleared off in the spring of 2005.

At 0.6 miles we have reached the top of the ridge and now begin a steep decline. As we hike down the hill watch your step as we go over loose rocks, ledge rock and some small cedar post placed across the trail to help with erosion.

After reaching the bottom, at 0.8 miles, the trail levels off for a while. We are now able to spend some time enjoying an easy hike looking at wildflowers and any wildlife that might be roaming around. Soon we cross another wet weather creek and the trail goes up hill for a short way and we come to an intersection at 1.0 miles.

The trail to the right is the way back to the parking lot. If you do go back to the parking lot at this point you will have hiked about 1.7 miles. But we want to continue hiking so we will take the trail to the left as we continue to follow the yellow and silver trail.

About 50 yards down the trail we see where the trail splits again. We will take the trail straight ahead as it goes slightly down hill. The trail to the right is the way we will be coming back in a little while.

We will follow the trail down the hill and cross a wet weather creek at 1.1 miles. The trail is now fairly level for awhile as we continue out through the woods.

Then at 1.3 miles we come out into a large opening. This is where the Yellow trail and Silver trail part ways. The Yellow trail will go to the left, down hill, and the Silver trail will go to the right, up hill. You guessed it. We will be going to the right, UPHILL! If there was ever a good time to have a horse, this is it! The climb is fairly steep with lots of loose rocks, so watch your step. As always, take your time, stop and rest as often as you need to and drink lots of water and before you know it, we will be at the top of the hill. Do stop about half way up and turn around for a SGV of the beautiful hills behind you.

Finally, at 1.5 miles the trail begins to level off. We will go across the top of the hill through the woods and at 1.9 miles the trail turns to the right and this time we get to go downhill!

The trail going down is pretty steep so be sure and watch your step. We don't want anyone to get hurt out here so far away from help. Then at 2.1 miles the trail begins to level off as we go around the side of the hill. Take time to notice the wildflowers. There are a lot of elephant ear plants along the trail.

After awhile the trail will go back down hill for a little ways and then begin to follow along side a creek. We will continue on through the woods, cross the creek and come to a trail intersection. This is where we were earlier when I said, "This is the way we will be coming back in a little while."

We will be taking the trail to the left as we begin to hike back to the trailhead. After about 50 yards the trail will separate again. The trail to the right is the way we came up earlier. We want to follow the trail straight ahead taking the time to enjoy the beautiful flowers along the way.

When we reach the 2.6 mile point the trail will go up hill slightly and then level off again at 2.8 miles. We are now walking along an old road that is shaded with a nice canopy of trees.

At 3.0 miles we are back to the first junction of the trail where we were at the beginning of our hike. We took the trail to the right earlier but now we want to continue straight ahead, slightly up hill, to the trailhead for a total hike of 3.1 miles.

BUSIEK PURPLE TRAIL

3.4 miles

GPS:	N 36' 51.841 W 93' 14.141
Trail Length:	3.4 mile loop
Trail Type:	Natural
Average Hiking Time:	1.5 - 2 hours
Rating:	Moderate
Calories	Burned: 690 – 920

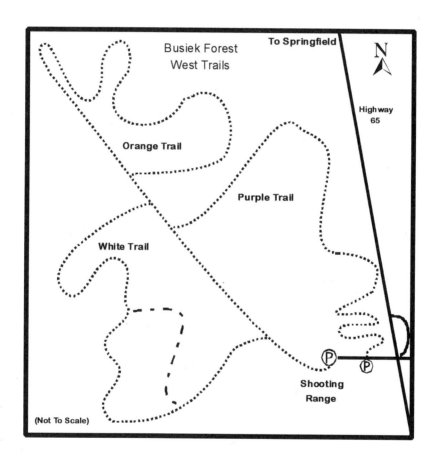

Busiek Forest West Trails

To Springfield

N

Highway 65

Orange Trail

Purple Trail

White Trail

Shooting Range

P P

(Not To Scale)

PURPLE TRAIL

DIRECTIONS TO TRAILHEAD

From highway 76, go north on highway 65 for 15.4 miles. You will see a brown information sign along the highway just before you get there. Turn right and follow the paved road down to the bottom of the hill. At the bottom of the hill you will turn right and go under the highway 65 bridge and past a rock quarry. On the right, just past the rock quarry, you will see a yellow conservation sign on a small tree and the trail going uphill. This is where we will begin the Purple Trail. The road does go back just a little bit further and dead ends with a metal bridge going over the creek to the shooting range and the trailheads for the White and Orange Trail. We will be coming back that way at the end of our hike. You can park anywhere in this area. The trail can be hiked in either direction but we believe it is easier if you go in a counter clockwise direction.

DESCRIPTION OF TRAIL

The trail begins by going up the trail by the yellow conservation sign, looking worse than it actually is. The trail originally went straight up the hill, but now it has several switchbacks that go up the side of the hill, which makes the trail a little bit longer but a whole lot easier to hike. If there is anyone at the shooting range it can be a little noisy but it will get quieter as we get closer to the top of the hill and into the woods.

As we are going uphill to the west you can see the parking lot and the shooting range down on your left. Then when we are going to the east you will be able to see highway 65 in the valley below. The view from up on the side of the hill is really beautiful, especially if you are here on an early morning watching the sun come up over the hills.

We are getting closer to the top, the gun shots, if any, are becoming more muffled and it has been a fairly easy hike because of the switchbacks. As we approach the 0.6 mile point, the trail will switch back to the east, facing highway 65, and we will be hiking along the edge of the woods where there are several SGV's along the way.

When we approach 1.0 mile we can again see highway 65,

the rock quarry down on the right and the trail will turn to the left as it goes into the woods.

The trail goes gradually uphill as we follow along an old road. Even though people do ride their horses up here they do not seem to ride the trails on this side of the highway as much as the other side, therefore the trails do not have as much loose rock and are easier to walk on.

After we reach the top of the hill the trail will be level for awhile, so enjoy the quiet and shade as we hike along the top of the ridge. Be on the lookout for deer, turkey, squirrels, wild-flowers or anything else you might see.

At 2.0 miles the trail comes into a small field which could have been an old home site at one time. If you look to the right there is a trail that goes a short distance to some private property and a couple of houses. As the trail turns to the left and begins to go downhill notice the big walnut trees on the right side of the trail. They have been here along time.

As we continue to gradually go downhill we will cross a wet weather creek at 2.3 miles. Watch your step, there are loose rocks on this part of the trail and we don't want anyone to twist an ankle!

We reach the bottom of the hill at 2.5 miles where you come to a trail intersection and an information sign. As you can see on the sign, this next part of the trail is shared by all three trails, so if you hike the White and Orange Trail you will hike this section each time. It is an easy and enjoyable hike and if you are here in the spring, early summer and fall you will get to see many beautiful wildflowers along the way.

So, as we head back to the trailhead, we will turn left at the sign and follow the trail as we go through the lovely Ozark valley.

At 2.6 miles the trail turns to the right, back into the woods and across a creek bed. We will continue to follow the trail as we cross the creek a couple more times. Then at 3.1 miles you will see a trail that takes off to the right. This is the beginning of the White Trail. We will stay to the left and at 3.4 miles we are at the bridge that takes us to the parking lot.

Pace yourself! Kids have a tendency to use up too much energy at the beginning of a hike and have to be carried back out. Have them slow down by having them look and examine the flowers, insects and whatever else you found along the way.

BUSIEK WHITE TRAIL

4.4 miles

GPS: N 36' 51.841 W 93' 14.141
Trail Length: 4.4 miles
Trail Type: Natural
Average Hiking Time: 3 hours
Rating: Moderate
Calories Burned: 1,380

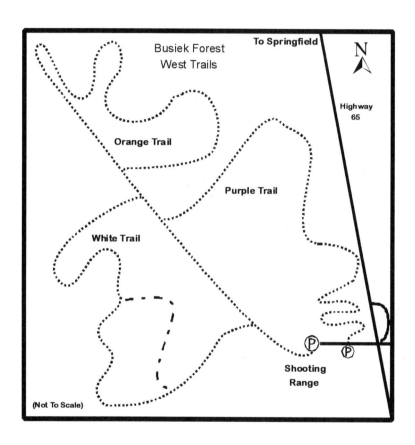

WHITE TRAIL

DIRECTIONS TO TRAILHEAD

From highway 76, go north on highway 65 for 15.4 miles. You will see a brown information sign along the highway just before you get there. Turn right and follow the paved road down to the bottom of the hill. At the bottom of the hill you will turn right and go under the highway 65 bridge and past a rock quarry. Just past the rock quarry the road dead ends at the parking area. As you come into the parking area you will see a metal bridge on your left. This takes you across the creek where you will see a shooting range on your left and the trailhead on your right.

DESCRIPTION OF TRAIL

The trail that we are going to hike will not follow the trail as laid out on the signs and in the official brochures. We are going to follow a trail that will be a little bit longer in length but, in our opinion, easier hiking. Either direction we go there is a steep hill that we have to hike up but the one we will take is more gradual, less loose rocks and is a lot better trail.

Most of this trail is easy to hike with only one place where it is fairly steep and it doesn't last very long. Most of our hike will be in the shade as we go through the woods, so it is a good trail to hike on those hot sunny days. We will cross some creeks so if there has been a lot of rain you will get your feet.

Let's begin by crossing over the bridge and taking the trail that takes off to the right. The hike begins under a covering of trees that filters the sun as it tries to shine through. This helps to keep us a little cooler but it also keeps the trail from drying out, so if it has rained at all in the past few days there will still be a few puddles we will have to go around, or through, along the way.

At 0.4 miles the trail will fork and we will take the trail to the left. The trail to the right is the way we will be coming back.

We will be following along the edge of a creek which we will be crossing from time to time along with some lesser wet weather creeks. The trail is fairly level as it rolls up and down through the bottom land. When Janet and I were here on a sunny June day there was a large wild rose bush on the opposite creek bank at about 0.7 miles, that was in full bloom and really beautiful. Seeing such beautiful flowers is one of the things that we enjoy about living and hiking in the Ozarks.

After hiking about 0.3 miles the trail will rise about ten feet above the creek and then come back down to the creek bed at 1.1 mile. Here is where the official trail takes off to the right, across the creek to the other side. You will see some white marks on a couple of trees and there should be a small hiking trail sign on a tree on the other side of the creek. You can go that direction if you want to but there will be a very steep, rocky climb up the side of the hill.

For the rest of us we will continue hiking the trail straight ahead along the creek and as we come to the 1.2 mile point in the trail you will see a fence and signs telling us we have reached the end of the public land and the beginning of private land. Be sure and not cross over the fence onto someone else's property. The trail will turn to the right and will cross the creek and follow the fence line for awhile. Soon, the trail leaves the fence line and turns to the right following a wet weather creek uphill.

At 1.3 miles we cross the creek and go back uphill to our left. The trail is kind of steep and will switchback up the hill for about 0.1 miles before it levels off and takes off through the woods. When you see the big oak tree with the white mark the worst part of the trail is over.

We will intersect with another trail at 1.8 miles. The trail to the left goes about 0.2 miles to private property. We will take the trail to the right and at 1.9 miles the trail comes to a "Y" intersection. The trail to the right is the way we would have come if we had taken the "official" trail earlier in our hike. So take the trail to the left as we head downhill.

We will hike along the top of the ridge for awhile and then gradually head on down the hill. This part of the trail looks like an old road. On your way down, on the right side of the trail, see if you can find the large oak tree with a big hole at the bottom of the trunk. Just after the large oak tree the trail will make a U turn to the left.

At 2.4 miles the trail will level off for a short distance and then turns to the right, goes down the hill and at the bottom the trail opens up, levels off and becomes narrower. We will cross a small creek and at 2.9 miles there will be a trail that goes to the left uphill. Stay on the main trail that continues straight ahead.

Just ahead, we will cross the main creek and intersect with the Orange Trail at 3.0 miles. Take the trail to the right. Then, at 3.3 miles, we see a trail sign on our left and this is where the Purple Trail joins the main trail back to the trailhead.

Continue to follow the trail straight ahead out through the field. As we come to 3.6 miles the trail will turn to the right into the woods, cross the creek and then turn back to the left.

We will cross back over the creek a couple more times and at 4.0 miles we will see a trail that takes off to the right. This is where we started the White Trail a few hours ago. This time we want to take the trail to the left as we go back to the trail-head at 4.4 miles.

BUSIEK ORANGE TRAIL

5.0 miles

GPS: N 36' 51.841   W 93' 14.141
Trail Length: 5.0 mile loop
Trail Type: Natural
Average Hiking Time: 3 hours
Rating: Moderate
Calories Burned: 1,380

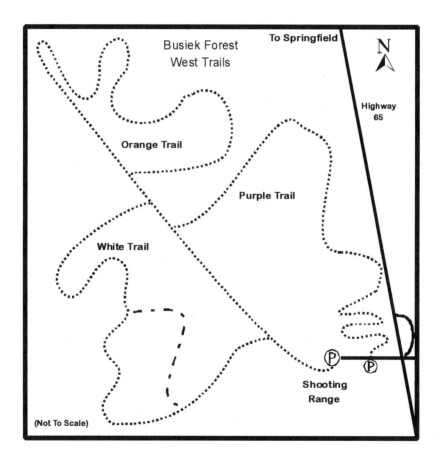

ORANGE TRAIL

DIRECTIONS TO TRAILHEAD

Follow the same directions as described in the White Trail.

DESCRIPTION OF TRAIL

After crossing the bridge the trail starts on our right, past the information sign, and begins as a leisurely walk through the woods as it follows along side of Camp creek. If it has rained recently the trail can be a little muddy but don't let mud and a few puddles keep you from hiking.

At 0.4 miles we will come to a "Y" in the trail. The trail to the left is the White Trail. We will take the trail to the right and soon come to a creek crossing at 0.5 miles. The creek is usually dry, except after a few days of rain. After crossing the creek take notice of the tall beautiful flowers growing along the creek and both sides of the trail. It is called mullein or common mullein. It is an interesting plant that has flowers growing in a tightly packed cluster on very tall stalks. The leaves are huge and soft to the touch. They have been used as diapers, wicks for lamps and candles and when infused with grease, used as torches.

After crossing the creek the trail will turn to the left and follow along the creek for a short distance and then cross back over the creek, staying in shade.

At 0.8 miles we go back over the creek and the trail turns to the left as it opens up into a field and we will be hiking in the sun for awhile as we leave our canopy of shade. If you like blackberries, and are here in late June and July, be on the lookout for patches along the trail, they sure are good!

As we approach the 1.0 mile point we come to an information sign on the right side of the trail. The trail that takes off to the right and goes uphill is the purple trail, so we will continue on the trail that goes straight ahead past the sign.

The trail remains level and out in the open. At 1.2 miles it will turn to the right, go a few feet, turn back to the left and go through some trees for a short distance before it opens back out into a field. There is a lesser trail on the left but we want to stay to the right.

Then at 1.4 miles there will be a trail that takes off to the left into the woods, this is the White Trail. We will follow the trail straight ahead as we continue going through the field. You can see where the Conservation Department has planted food for the wildlife to enjoy.

As we approach the 1.6 mile point there will be a large steel pipe about 6½ feet in diameter on the right side of the trail. I have been told that this was left over from the previous owner of the land who was gong to use it for some project he had planned. Not knowing what to do with it or how to get it out the Conservation Department has just left it alone. After we pass the pipe we will cross a wet weather creek and there is small blackberry patch on the right. After going through another food plot the trail turns to the right, crosses a creek and then back to the left.

At 2.1 miles the trail seems to come to an abrupt end. We are at the end of the public land and the trail to the left, that has a no hiking sign, leads to private property. This is the end of the level hiking for awhile. The trail ahead is not bad. It does have some hills but none of them are really steep. If you have already hike the Silver or Yellow Trails on the other side of highway 65 this trail is easy. If you do not want to hike any hills, and just wanted a nice easy hike, you can turn around and follow the trail back to the trailhead for a hike of 4.2 miles. But if you want to complete the trail let's take the trail to the right as it begins to go uphill.

The uphill climb is not steep or long and soon levels off as we follow an old road. There will be a series of going uphill for awhile and then leveling off and then back uphill again until we reach the top. This helps the hike from becoming too steep. At one point we will come out into a glade. After going through the glade the trail will turn to the right where it takes a small dip as we cross a wet weather creek at 2.6 miles. After crossing the creek we will go uphill and go to the right where it levels off for a while. Then it will turn to the left back uphill.

If you look to your right you can catch glimpses of the Ozark hills and the valley below. It is a really great view after the leaves are off the trees. On our left are some ledge rock outcroppings.

We will be going steadily uphill as the trail continues to wind its way back and forth to the top of the hill. It does get a little steeper as we get closer to the top but before you know it we have reached the top, at 2.9 miles. Just as soon as we reach the top of the hill we begin our journey back down the other side.

As we go down the hill be sure and watch your step as there are loose rocks that you can slip on if you are not careful. After going downhill for awhile the trail will level off before it turns to the left and goes downhill some more.

At 3.1 miles the trail splits. The trail to the right is a shortcut down the side of the hill back to the main trail. The trail that goes straight ahead is the main trail and is a little longer but it is not as steep. It makes no difference which one you take they both get you to the bottom of the hill.

As we get to the bottom of the hill, at 3.2 miles, the worst of the trail is over. See, that wasn't so bad! You got to see some beautiful scenery, get your heart rate up and burned off all of those calories! And it is a lot more fun than that tread mill!

The trail remains fairly level as we go through the woods back to the main trail. Just before the main trail we will turn to the left, out into the open and downhill slightly to the information sign we had come to earlier in our hike. Turn left at the sign and follow the trail back to the trailhead for a hike of 5.0 miles.

"A vigorous five mile walk will do more good for an unhappy but otherwise healthy adult than all the medicine and psychology in the world."

Paul Dudley White

DRURY - MINCY CONSERVATION AREA

The Drury – Mincy Conservation Area is composed of 5,599 acres. The area was first leased in 1939 and then purchased by the Commission in 1987. It is named for an early landowner Frank Drury and the settlement of Mincy.

Around 1900 Missouri's deer population was down to about 14 herds and one of those herds was in the Drury-Mincy area. So it became the Conservation Department's first deer refuge and was successful in restoring deer herds throughout Missouri.

Then in the 1960's the Drury-Mincy area was used to restore wild turkeys throughout the state. Both programs were successful in restoring deer and turkey in all parts of the state where large numbers are harvested each season by hunters.

Camping is allowed only in designated areas and is limited to 14 consecutive days in a 30 day period. There are no fireworks, ATV's, or target shooting. Dogs are to be on leashes except when being trained or used for hunting. There is an archery range located on the left just past the campground that we will go past on our way to the trailhead. So if you have your archery equipment be sure to stop and see how well you can do.

Bike riding is allowed in this area on any road that is open to vehicles. Janet and I will ride the gravel road that leads down to the Old Bee Creek School and also ride Gunnison road from the bridge until the road turns to the left and begins a long climb up hill. We then turn around and come back. We do like to ride but we haven't gotten into hilling climbing, yet!

"Climb the mountains and get their good tidings. Nature's peace will flow into you as sunshine flows into trees. The winds will blow their own freshness into you, and the storms their energy, while cares will drop off like autumn leaves."

John Muir

BEAR CAVE TRAIL

2.0 miles

GPS:	N 36' 32.728 W 93' 06.751
Trail Length:	2 mile round trip
Trail Type:	Natural
Average Hiking Time:	1.5 - 2 hours round trip
Rating:	Moderate
Calories Burned:	690 – 920

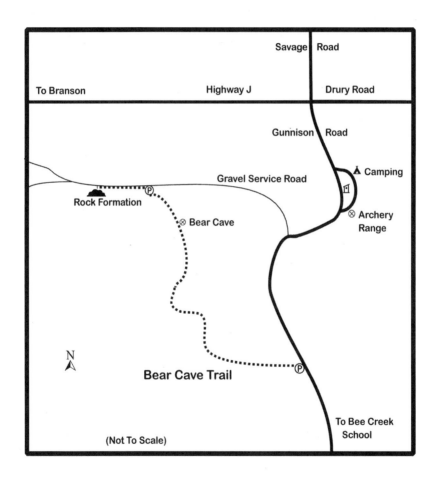

DIRECTIONS TO TRAILHEAD

From highway 65/76 to the trailhead is 12.5 miles. We will go east on 76 and head down the hill toward downtown Branson. You will need to get in the right hand lane and at the bottom of the hill, turn right at the stop light. Follow highway 76 /business 65 as you go through town and cross the bridge over Lake Taneycomo.

At the end of the bridge we will turn left, staying on highway 76. From the bridge go 5.5 miles to highway J just past the school you will see on your right in Kirbyville.

Stay on highway J for 5.5 miles to the old town of Mincy. At the intersection we will turn right onto Gunnison road (J-40).

At 0.7 miles you will see a campground with restrooms on your left. At the other end of the campground there is an archery range.

Then at 1.2 miles there is a gravel road on your right that turns back and heads up hill 0.3 miles to the trailhead on your left.

While you are here be sure and take some time to see the large rock formation that seems to grow out of the ground just past the trailhead on your left.

If the gate is closed, continue on Gunnison road and you will see a small parking lot and the trailhead on your right. You will then be following the trail description in reverse.

DESCRIPTION OF TRAIL

The trail is well marked and begins to the left of the parking area. It begins by heading out in the woods and gradually going down hill. At 0.1 mile on our left we come to where the trail gets its name, Bear Cave. The opening is not very big and you will have to crawl in. If you do decide to explore the cave be sure and follow the warnings and let someone else know what you are doing. The cave opens up into a bigger room where you can stand up. To the right is a little opening that you can crawl into but doesn't go back very far. You can walk most of the way to the back of the cave but is tight in a couple of spots. The floor is clay and can be muddy at times. I did not measure the total distance to the back of the cave but I would guess around 100 feet. If you go in, have fun, but be careful!

The trail continues down hill past the cave and turns to the left and at 0.2 miles we cross a wet weather creek as the trail levels off and follows along the edge of the creek.

Then at 0.3 miles we cross over the top of a small falls and go back across the creek. Notice the large root that sticks out of the ground. For some good pictures of the creek you need to be here just after a good rain. After we cross the creek the trail opens up into a small glade and then goes back into the woods and crosses back over the creek at 0.4 miles.

We now continue to follow along the creek as we gently head down hill. Then at 0.5 miles we once again cross back over the creek over another small falls then the trail goes slightly uphill through another small glade. One spring day, while hiking the trail, I jumped two turkeys in this field and watched them fly down hill through the trees. Always try to be fairly quiet as you go through the woods and be on the look out for any wildlife you might see. Janet and I have seen all kinds of wildlife while hiking, except a bear. Maybe one day we will get to see one of them! But not to close!

There will be a log bench on our right just after we cross the creek. On one of my hiking trips I noticed that the top log of the bench was gone. I looked around trying to see what happened to it. Sure enough, it was down the hill at the bottom of the creek bed. So I got down into the creek (it was dry) and wrestled the log back up the hill and put it back in its place. So do me a favor and sit down and enjoy my labors. I hope it is still there!

As we continue on up through the glade the trail does get a little steeper, although it doesn't get too steep. Time your time and look out across the beautiful Ozark hills as we go on up the hill. And don't forget to look down at the pretty wild flowers growing in the glade.

At 0.7 miles, at the top of the hill, we come to a large outcropping of rocks and a SGV as you look out to your right. And, as luck would have it, there are also two more log benches where you can sit down and rest!

When you are ready to go follow the trail on through the rocks, around the hill and back into the woods. The trail will gradually go down hill and at 1.0 miles we come to the other trailhead and parking lot located on Gunnison road.

Now, just follow the trail back to your car for a total hike of 2.0 miles.

OLD BEE CREEK SCHOOL AND CEMETERY

After your hike, if you want to do some more exploring, continue on down Gunnison road until you come to the bridge at the bottom of the hill. On your way you will see some old concrete buildings on your right; this is the site of an old charcoal plant. When you come to the bridge take the gravel road just before it to the left. Immediately after the second creek crossing there will be a small sign on your left saying Old Bee Creek School. Take the path up the hill and after going a short distance you will come to the foundation of the Old School. The cemetery is just to the right of the Old School. On your way back out there will be a small path to your left that leads up to another headstone.

If you want, go ahead and stay on the gravel road and follow it on up the creek until you come to where the road turns to the left and heads uphill. This is where you will need to turn around and go back (unless you have a four wheel truck) because the road is washed out.

Janet's dad use to own 40 acres starting at this point and continuing uphill. We did a lot of hunting, hiking and camping in this area back then.

EMPIRE DISTRICT ELECTRIC COMPANY PARK

(Ozark Beach Recreation Area)

EMPIRE PARK TRAIL

GPS:	N 36' 51.563 W 93' 04.612
Trail Length:	2.2 miles
Trail Type:	Paved
Average Hiking Time:	1 hour
Rating:	Easy
Calories Burned:	310

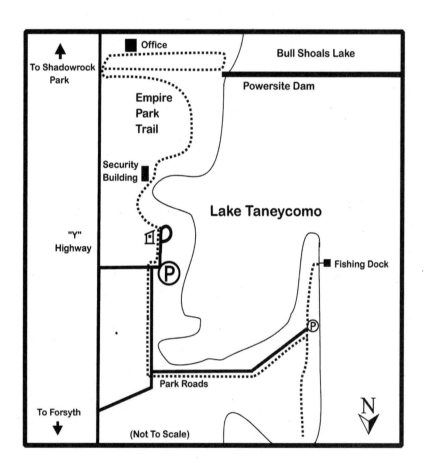

DIRECTIONS TO TRAILHEAD

Total distance to trailhead is 17.2 miles from highway 76/65. Go east on highway 76 toward downtown Branson and go down the hill to the stop light, staying in the right lane, turn right at the stop light and continue on to the other side of the Lake Taneycomo Bridge at 1.2 miles. We will go to the left staying on highway 76. Follow highway 76 until we have come to the other end of the Bull Shoals Bridge at 13.2 miles. At the stop sign turn left onto highway 160, crossing over the Swan Creek Bridge and come to another stop sign at 14.3 miles. Turn left onto highway Y, go another 1.2 miles (15.5 miles total) and turn into the scenic overlook on the right. This gives you a SGV of the lower end of Lake Taneycomo. The houses you see on the other side of the lake is accessed off of T highway which takes off of highway 76 back toward Branson.

When you have finished enjoying the view, turn right as you leave the scenic view area and go another 1.7 miles down to Empire Park. We will take the third road on the right that goes into the park. This is the boat launch area and where the restrooms and pavilion are located. We have now traveled 17.2 miles from highway 76/65. This is where we will begin our hike.

DESCRIPTION OF TRAIL

The trail goes in two directions from the parking lot. We will begin by taking the trail that goes between the restrooms and the lake. This part of the trail is concrete. It will go around the edge of the cove, below an old office building and out through a grassy area with large beautiful trees along the edge of the lake.

At 0.4 miles we come to the sidewalk that leads up to the dam. Turn to the right and follow it up the steps to the overlook. From here you get a good view of Lake Taneycomo and Empire Park. Straight ahead we can see the water as it flows over the dam and the beginning of Bull Shoals Lake.

As you stand there looking at the water fall over the dam keep in mind that at times of high water these two lakes have been almost at the same level. Of course, when this happens, Shadow Rock Park which is about 2.3 miles downstream is under water. The present site of Shadow Rock Park is the location where the town of Forsyth was originally built. But after the building of Bull Shoals Dam, in Bull Shoals Arkansas in 1952, the town was forced to move to higher ground to its present location so as to avoid being flooded.

When you are ready to leave the overlook, take the steps down to the right toward the bottom of the dam. At the bottom of the steps you can look back at the dam and the headwaters of Bull Shoals Lake.

As we continue our hike take the sidewalk up toward the old rock house that is used as an office for the security guards. Follow the sidewalk as it goes around the building and turn to the left when we get to the front of the office. The trail to the right will soon be done and will go about 2.5 miles to Shadow Rock Park. If it is completed and you go to the old Swan Creek bridge and back add another 5.0 miles and 740 calories to your hike.

We are now back to the concrete walkway that we were on earlier and will follow it back to the parking lot for a total round trip of one mile.

After we get back to the parking lot you might want to go down to the boat ramp and walk out on the boat dock. Just watch for people loading and unloading their boats. When you are ready we will walk up to the service road above the parking lot and take it to the left. This will take us on around to the other side of the cove. This little cove is a good place to sit and watch the birds. There are Great White Egrets, Great Blue Herons, Canadian Geese, ducks and a variety of other birds. If you are really lucky you may even spot a Bald Eagle.

Once we are on the other side of the cove we will go to the left and out on the peninsula. From here you can look out across the cove to your left and see your car parked on the other side. In front of you is a couple of picnic areas and to the right a fishing dock. This is really a beautiful area of Lake Taneycomo.

We will now go back across the parking lot and go to the left of the big sycamore tree. Here you will find a 1,000 foot walking path. Follow this walkway as we go along the edge of the lake. There are some flowers and bushes along the shore that have been good places to photograph flowers, butterflies, dragon-flies and bees. At the end of the trail you will come to a bench. From here we will turn around, follow the trail back out to the big sycamore tree, turn left and head back to the parking lot. When we get back to the trailhead we have walked a total of 2.2 miles.

"When preparing to travel, lay out all of your clothes and all of your money. Then take half of the clothes and twice the money."

Susan Heller

Ruth and Paul Henning
Forest Conservation Area

This 1,534 acre conservation area was sold to the Missouri Conservation Department by Ruth and Paul Henning. Paul was a well known Hollywood writer and is most noted as the creator of "The Beverly Hillbillies", "Petticoat Junction" and Executive Producer of the "Green Acres" show in the 1960's. While visiting the Branson area Paul and Ruth noticed the rapid development of the Branson area and was concerned that it was ruining the beautiful Ozark Scenery that Branson was known for. So they began to buy the land that is now the **Ruth and Paul Henning Conservation Area**. Ruth noted that they resisted many offers by developers to sell the land for millions of dollars. Instead, they chose to sell it to the Missouri Conservation Department for a fraction of what they could have received on the open market.

We want to thank Ruth and Paul for their foresight and generosity in making this land available for all to enjoy for generations to come. Sadly, Paul passed away on March 25, 2005 at the age of 93.

There are five trails located in the area that takes you from the top of a forty foot tower overlooking the city of Branson, out through the forest and glades, and down to the headwaters of the beautiful Roark creek. This is the same creek that runs past Stockstill Park and empties into Lake Taneycomo just north of the Branson Landing.

The five trails are the Dewey Bald Trail, Glade Trail, Streamside Trail, Shane's Shortcut Trail and the Homestead Trail. You can enjoy a short hike on the paved Dewey Bald Trail up to the lookout tower, hike all five trails together or hike anything in between. Each trail is unique and has its own beauty and history giving you the opportunity to spend an hour or all day hiking and sightseeing.

Even though there are five different trails listed, the Streamside Trail and Shane's Shortcut Trail are not hiked by themselves. So we are going to combine the Glade Trail and the Streamside Trail into one trail and Shane's Shortcut Trail is included in the Dewey – Homestead Trail. Therefore, we will describe four different trails;

Dewey Bald Trail
Glade and Streamside Trail
Homesteader's Trail
Dewey – Homestead Trail

DEWEY BALD TRAIL

0.5 miles

GPS:	N 36' 39.590 W 93' 17.728
Trail Length:	0.5 miles
Trail Type:	Paved
Average Hiking Time:	20-30 minutes
Rating:	Easy
Calories Burned:	160

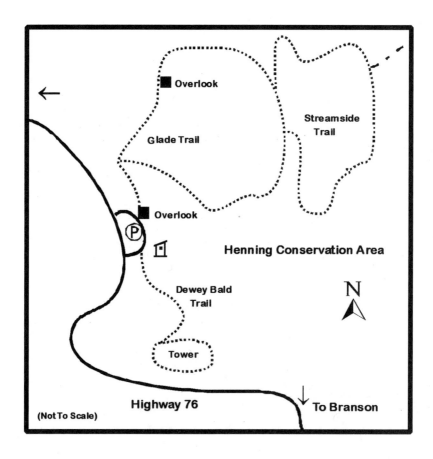

In spring you will see dogwood trees and lots of wild flowers and birds all along the trail. The trail is paved and is wheel chair accessible although it is a little bit of an incline up to the tower. There is no camping or fires in this area. There are restrooms to your right when you first enter the parking area. Since there is no drinking water on the trails be sure and bring plenty of your own, especially in the summer. Pets are permitted only on leash. Be sure and bring your camera and binoculars. Just a word of caution, there is a lot of poison ivy along the way so be sure and keep the kids on the trail.

DIRECTIONS TO TRAILHEAD

This trail is located on Highway 76 at the West end of Branson about one mile from the Shepherd of the Hills Farm. The distance, if you can take Highway 76 from downtown Branson all the way out to the Henning Forest is 5.1 miles. This route is ok if you are going early in the morning but most of the time Highway 76 is usually pretty crowded. Another way to get there from downtown Branson is to go north on highway 65 and go about 0.7 miles and take the highway 248 exit. At the stop light turn left onto highway 248. Stay in the right lane and at 2.8 miles highway 248 turns to the right. Now get in the left lane and turn left at the next stop light onto the Shepherd of the Hills Expressway. Stay on the Expressway and when you see the I-Max Theater at 6.0 miles get in the right lane. The stop light ahead is highway 76. Turn right onto highway 76 and at 7.0 miles you will see the entrance to the Ruth and Paul Henning Conservation Area on your right. If you are hiking the Dewey Bald Trail find a place to park by the restrooms, for the other trails go on down the parking lot to the overlook. The Homestead Trail can be accessed from this trailhead but to just hike it by itself you will need to follow the directions found under the description for the Homestead Trail.

DESCRIPTION OF TRAIL

As soon as you come into the parking lot there will be restrooms on your right. The trailhead is located to the right of the restrooms. The trail begins to wind its way uphill. It is a gradual incline and if you do need to stop and take a rest there are four benches that are located along the trail as you hike your way to the observation tower. When you come to the third bench you will notice that the trail takes off in two directions. This is where the trail loops around the tower. We want to stay to the right as we will be coming down the other side on our way back from the tower.

As you approach the fourth bench the trail opens up at the top of the hill and there, in front of you, is the observation tower. Go ahead and head to the top!!! You have come this far, be brave, don't stop now! It is only 55 steps to the top but what a view!

You can see a large part of Branson from up here. To your left you can see the Red Roof Mall. Just past the Red Roof Mall you can see the College of the Ozarks and the airport which is on the other side of Lake Taneycomo. Directly in front of you is Celebration City. The road in front of Celebration City is Highway 376 which connects Highway 76 with Highway 265. The hills you see way off in the distance are located in Arkansas. To your right, and kind of behind you, is the Shepherd of the Hills Tower. This is definitely a SGV!

What else can you identify from up here? I hope you brought your camera and binoculars!

As we leave the tower we will take the trail to the left and begin our hike back down to the parking lot. As we head down we will again pass by four benches. At the second bench we are back to where the trail intersected on our way up. This time we will turn to the right and head on down hill. Take your time and enjoy your hike. Soon you are back to the parking lot.

The trailhead for the Glade and Streamside Trail begins at the observation deck at the other end of the parking lot.

To help keep the parks and trails clean and in good shape stay on the trails. Don't be tempted to cut across the switchbacks. They are there to help prevent the trail from eroding.

GLADE AND STREAMSIDE TRAIL   1.5 miles

GPS:	N 36' 39.590 W 93' 17.728
Trail Length:	1.5 miles
Trail Type:	Natural
Average Hiking Time:	1.5 to 2 hours
Rating:	Moderate
Calories Burned:	690 – 920

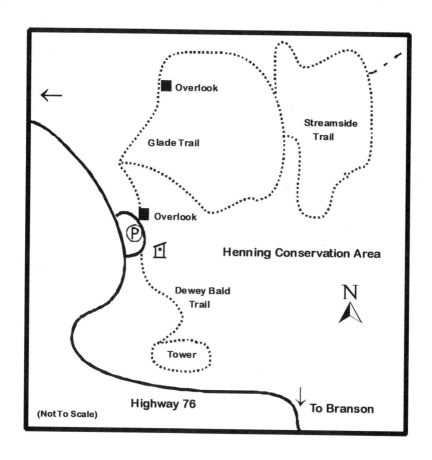

The Glade Trail is 1.1 miles and the Streamside Trail is 0.4 miles. We are going to combine the two trails into one for a total of 1.5 miles. Through parts of the trail you will be going through woods and bottomland. But the most impressive part of the hike will be the open desert-like areas known as glades or "balds". Make sure you and bring your camera and binoculars. When you get to the parking lot you can tune your radio to AM 1630 for information concerning the history and folklore of the area. The first part of the trail is pretty level so if you want an easy hike, you could go out to the second overlook deck and back again for a total hike of 0.8 miles. The rest of the trail past the second overlook is rated moderate.

DIRECTIONS TO TRAILHEAD

Follow the directions as found under the Dewey Bald Trail.

DESCRIPTION OF TRAIL

At the overlook take a few minutes to look around and enjoy the beautiful view of the White Cedar Bald. When you are ready the trailhead begins down the steps to the left. The first part of the trail is easy going as we walk under a canopy of trees. A little ways up on our right you will be able to see the glade through a small opening in the trees. The white cylinder water tower off in the distance is the Meadow Ridge Subdivision located on Sycamore Log Church Road off of highway 248.

At 0.1 miles we will come to an intersection. We want to continue straight ahead over the two small wooden foot bridges. The trail to our right is the way we will be coming back. As we continue to hike along the side of the hill we will have the forest on our left and the glade on our right.

At 0.3 miles there will be a large opening on our right and a good view of the glade area and in the distance, Branson. Can you see the Red Roof Mall or the Grand Palace?

As we continue on around the trail there will be several SGV as we look out over the glades. But don't forget to look down along the trail once in awhile for some beautiful wild flowers and maybe a little lizard or two.

If you hear a train whistle off in the distance it is coming from the Frisco train ride at Silver Dollar City.

At 0.4 miles we come to another overlook deck and this

one has a bench! Sit down, relax and enjoy the view! This is definitely a SGV!!!

I think this is one of the best views in Branson, don't you? The glade we are in is Boulder Bald. The ridge to our left is South Cox's Bald and down at the bottom to our right is Long Bald.

When you are ready, continue the trail on around the glade. We will now start to wind our way down hill over some ledge rock as we go along the bottom of Boulder Bald. Watch your step. When you get toward the bottom of the glade if you look up to your right you will see the overlook we just left a few minutes ago. Soon the trail goes back into the woods and at 0.6 miles we come to a bench on our right.

The trail continues in and out of the glade and at 0.7 miles we come to the intersection of the Streamside Trail. If you want to head on back up to the trailhead go straight and follow the trail up the hill. Stay on the main trail and it will connect with the first intersection we came to at 0.1 miles from the first overlook. Turn left at this intersection and back to the parking lot for a total hike of 1.1 miles.

But we will take the trail to the left as we follow the Streamside Trail. The trail will go in and out of the woods and glades and cross over two small wooden foot bridges. We will follow along side a wet weather stream on our left and will soon come to a bench. Next, we see Shane's Shortcut Trail take off to our left as it connects to the Homesteader's Trail. This is the trail you will take if you hike the Dewey Bald – Homestead Trail. But, for now, we will continue straight ahead and follow the Streamside Trail.

The trail now follows along side another little stream and crosses a couple more small wooden foot bridges. As we come out of the woods we will be at the intersection of the Glade Trail at 1.1 miles. We will follow the trail to our left and begin our hike back up the hill.

As the trail winds its way back up to the top we will be going in and out of the glade and the woods. A short distance up the trail, in a section of trees, there will be a bench sitting in the shade so stop and rest awhile. Then the trail will open back up into the glade where you need to watch your step on some of the loose ledge rock, especially if they are wet.

We will then come to another bench. STOP and REST! Take some time to set, relax and enjoy the peace and quiet. It is hard to imagine that you are only a couple of miles from the hustle and bustle of highway 76. Do you see any birds, lizards, or flowers? This is the roughest section of the whole trail but if you take your time and drink your water you will make it in fine shape.

As we get closer to the top we will see a couple of lesser trails taking off to our left. Just ignore these and stay on the main trail and before you know it we will be back at the intersection of the Glade and Streamside Trail where we were earlier. Take the trail to the left and we will head back to the parking lot for a total hike of 1.5 miles.

HOMESTEADER'S TRAIL

3.7 miles

GPS:	N 36' 41.017 W 93' 17.238
Trail Length:	3.7 mile loop
Trail Type:	Natural
Average Hiking Time:	3 – 3.5 hours
Rating:	Moderate
Calories Burned:	1,380 – 1,610

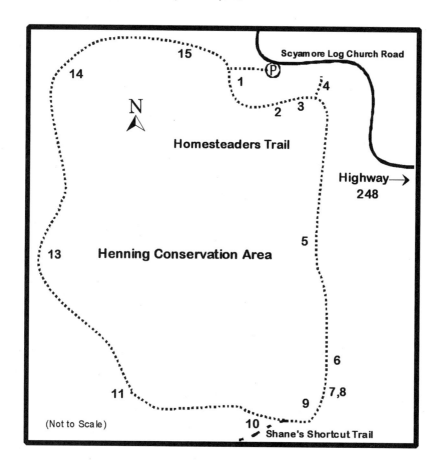

This is one of the most interesting trails that we have hiked. It is rich in history and gives us a glimpse of how rugged and determined the early homesteaders were who settled in this part of the country.

The remains that are left are from the old settlement of Garber. Along the way you will see remnants of old barns, houses, stores and wells.

The Missouri Department of Conservation puts out a brochure named "Henning Homesteaders Trail" that describes what you will see as you hike the trail. Sometimes you can find one in a box on the trail head sign, but don't count on it. If you don't have one, don't worry, because we will use the information from the brochure, published by the Missouri Department of Conservation, to describe the points of interest along the way. There are fifteen marker posts along the trail that are used to locate historical sites and other points of interest.

Located about a mile before you get to the trail is an interesting site that is not on the trail, the Old Sycamore Log Church. This old log cabin church still hold services every Sunday morning with 15-20 people in attendance. If you would like to stop and look around go ahead. All that we ask is that you do not disturb anything in and around the building. If you need to use the restrooms, they are out back!

DIRECTIONS TO TRAILHEAD

The distance from Branson to the trailhead is about 11.5 miles. From highway 76 go north on highway 65 for 4.5 miles to highway 465 (High Road) and turn left (west) onto highway 465. Go another 3.0 miles to the highway 248 turn off, which will be on your right. We will turn left onto highway 248 and go about 0.2 miles and turn right onto Sycamore Log Church Road. At 2.3 miles down this road you will come to the church on the right side of the road. Just past the church the road narrows to one lane, goes under a railroad trestle, and makes a sharp turn to the right. The road under the railroad trestle is one lane and makes a sharp turn to the right so be sure and go slow and watch for oncoming traffic. At 0.4 miles from the church, just before you cross the creek, you will see a parking lot on the left. The trailhead starts on the other side of the low water bridge.

To hike this trail along with the other trails in the area see the Dewey Bald – Homestead Trail description.

DESCRIPTION OF TRAIL

The clear stream that goes under the low water bridge is Roark Creek. This is the same creek that runs past Stockstill Park and enters Lake Taneycomo just north of the Branson Landing. One day there will be a trail along Roark Creek from the Branson Landing, on Lake Taneycomo, to the town of Reeds Spring. The plans are to have it finished in three to four years. We begin the trail by going across the bridge and heading up the steps. There you will see the trail split. We will go to the left and hike the trail as it is described in the brochure.

The trail follows above and along Roark Creek and crosses over some wet weather streams. There are some loose rocks so watch your step.

Just before we come to marker **post #1,** which is located by some sycamore trees at 0.2 miles, the trail will drop down to the edge of the creek. You can easily identify a sycamore tree by its white, "bleached" upper branches and loose bark. Since sycamore trees like lots of water a row of white trees was used by the early settlers as a good indication that water was near by. Maybe these are some of the same trees that drew the attention of the homesteaders that settled this part of Roark Creek.

The trail continues through the bottom land if you look around you will see some beautiful wild flowers, especially in the spring.

At 0.3 miles, on our left, we come to **marker #2,** the site of the old Stewart Store. George Stewart owned the two story building and it served the small town of Garber by being the center of trading and a place to socialize. People would come here to buy things such as salt, cotton, and meats. They could also trade and sell their surplus items like eggs or cream. Most of the items that were bought and traded came from the big city of Springfield.

In 1906 a record flood flowed over the banks of the creek and destroyed the store. The store was rebuilt and in 1920 the concrete wall that is in front of you was built to help keep the store from being flooded again. But ironically, it was a fire that destroyed the store for the final time in the late 1920's.

At the end of the concrete wall the trail goes across a dry (except after a hard rain) creek bed. On the other side, to your right, is a path that takes you to **marker #3** at 0.4 miles. This is the site of the Cox home. James Cox was listed as one of the Cox children in the 1840 census of this township. In the 1870 census, James Cox, 38 and his wife Ann, 33, had eight children between the ages of 2-15. Their homestead had a small corral and a hand dug well which was located next to their house. If you continue past the marker you will come to the old well. The children probably attended Dewey Grove School. In those days the children usually attended only about three months out of the year because there was so much work that had to be done around the house.

Coming back out to the main trail go to the right. Be on the lookout for three big old cedar posts next to the left side of the trail. You can see nails sticking out of them and one has a metal pipe stuck in the top. These may be the remains of the old corral.

At 0.5 miles we come to another split in the trail. For now let's go to the left. This path leads us to **marking post #4.** Here you can see the remains of an old pole barn that was built by Mr. Highford after he purchased the Cox farm in the 1920's. The barn was used to store the hay that was raised along the creek bottomland. You can go on down the trail for a better view of the remains of the old barn. If you follow this trail for 0.1 miles you will come to an open field.

After you are finished looking around go back to the main trail and go left as we begin a gradual hike uphill. It is a little steep with some erosion, so take your time and watch your step. This is an old road that is still used by the conservation department.

After about 0.2 miles the trail will level off then on your right, at 0.9 miles, we will see **marker #5.** Here you can see several cedar trees that are common throughout southwest Missouri. There are two types that grow in this area, red cedar and white cedar. Red cedar with its red, aromatic, rot resistant wood was valuable especially for fence post. Of the two types of trees it is the most common and grows in the typical Christmas tree shape. The white cedar is valuable for its soft light colored wood and is used for making pencils. Its shape is more rounded than that of the red cedar.

There were a lot of cedar trees harvested from this area between the years 1945 to 1948. You can still see some of the old stumps. During the Depression the locals would cut the cedars and haul them to the Gretna Railroad (near the charcoal plant on the Shepherd of the Hills Expressway) where they were paid a penny for each log. What a way to make a living!

The trail continues to go uphill and soon we come to a clearing as we go under some power lines. If you look to your right you can see the Shepherd of the Hills Lookout Tower located on highway 76 between Branson and Silver Dollar City.

Soon after we go back in the woods, at 1.3 miles, we come to **marker #6** on our left. This is the site of the old Jones house. Here you can see the row of cedar trees lining the road as they did years ago. The rock piles are the remains of the fireplaces, one on each end of the house. The pile on the left is larger. The logs were part of the kitchen. At one time this was a large, two story house.

On your left, at 1.4 miles, we come to **marker #7.** This is the location of the old Isaacs place. Reuben Isaacs was the temporary Taney County Sheriff from July 18 to September 1, 1889. He was appointed after Sheriff Galba Branson was shot to death by the Baldknobbers (a vigilante group) during a picnic on July 4, 1889. The metal pipe that you see is the casing of a well that was drilled in the early 1900's. The rock pile to the right was the fireplace.

Just past the Isaacs home site we see **marker #8.** This is the Pine Plantation. This is a short side trip of 0.2 miles. Follow the trail to the left and see what remains of an old field that had been cleared for farming then left to revegetate on its own. When the field was cleared at least one pine was left on the edge of the field and the seeds from that tree produced the other pine trees that you see today. The shortleaf pine is the only pine tree native to Missouri. They were very important to the early settlers for their use as lumber and railroad ties.

As we come out to the main trail and turn left we see a conservation sign ahead of us pointing that the trail turns to the right.

Just after we leave the old road and turn to the right, at 1.5 miles, we see a hand dug well at **marker #9.** Can you imagine digging a well about 25-30 feet deep in this rocky soil? It was quite a feat of engineering, strength and determination. As the well was dug, the walls were lined with rocks, set in place, so the well would not cave in.

As we continue, the trail remains level for a while and then begins to go downhill. At the bottom we will cross a creek (which is usually dry, except just after a rain) and come upon "Shane's Shortcut Trail" to our left. This is a 0.3 mile trail that connects the Homesteaders Trail with the Streamside and Glade Trail that begins off of highway76.

We will stay on the Homesteaders Trail so continue straight ahead. The trail will leave the creek and head uphill for awhile before it comes back alongside another creek. The trail goes right along the edge of the creek and it is a few feet to the creek bed below, so be careful in this area, especially if you have children.

At 2.1 miles we come to **marker #10** and a water fall. That is if it has rained recently. There are several water falls like this throughout the Ozarks. The water flows over the limestone and after years of erosion you have the creeks, valleys and cliffs so common in the Ozark Mountains.

The trail will go across the top of the falls and up the hill through the woods. At 2.3 miles the trail will open up into Cox's Glade where we have **marker #11.** (No marker #11 last time I was here). Glades, or Balds as they are sometimes called, are open, grassy areas that are usually found on the southern slopes of hills. These areas are unique because of their blend of desert and prairie conditions and you will find a large variety of plants and animals not usually found in the Midwest. If you look closely you may even find a cactus or two.

These glades, though hardy, are also very fragile because of the thin layer of soil that covers the ground. That is why we must be careful and stay on the trails so as to limit erosion.

One of the biggest threats to the glades is cedar trees. They will take over a glade if left unchecked and one of the best ways to manage a glade is with fire. The Missouri Department of Conservation will set controlled burns and cut down cedar trees to help maintain the glades in this area.

After going through the edge of the glade the trail now goes back into the woods for awhile before we go under power lines and back into the woods again. As we approach 2.5 miles, be on the lookout for **marker #12** which will be on our left. This is the site on the Newt Cox house. Newt owned 160 acres and built the house here around the early 1900's. Newt married Millie Garber, who was a member of the family that home-steaded the bald to the Northwest in the 1890's. Notice the large Oak trees that lined the drive to their house. You can still see the cut rock that was used for the foundation of the house.

Mille (Penmillie was her real name) was the first Postmaster of the town of Garber. The Post Office was just up the hill behind the house. Later the Post Office was moved when the town of Garber was relocated in 1907. At that time J.K. Ross (Old Matt in the book "The Shepherd of the Hills") became Postmaster.

A little further up the trail we will see some rock piles on our right. These are the rocks that were moved to help clear the land. Even today, if you want a yard or garden in this part of the country, it is a constant job of moving rocks.

We soon come to a clearing as we cross under more power lines. The trail enters the woods on the other side and on our left we come to **marker #13,** at 2.9 miles.

The large cedar trees mark the entrance to an old field. The barbed wire imbedded in the post shows that the fence has been here a long time. It is believed that Newt Cox's son was the one that cultivated the field and then left it to return back to natural growth around 1930 or 1931.

If you compare the trees on each side of the fence, you can

see the outline of the old field. Notice the variety of the size of the trees that are outside the old field and how uniform the trees are inside the old field. Janet and I are not sure but we think the field was on the left side of the fence in front of marker #13. What do you think?

As the trail continues between the large cedar trees we will be following the old road that was used by these early settlers. If you stop and are quiet for awhile you can almost imagine the horses and wagons as they traveled up and down the road.

This part of the trail is easy going as it goes slightly down-hill and winds through some large oak and cedar trees. In the spring you will see some dogwoods with their pretty white blossoms. It is so quiet and peaceful as we continue down the trail.

After awhile the trail will narrow and turn to the right as we go around an old fence. It will continue on down hill and then on the right at 3.3 miles we will see marker **post #14.** This is the site of the old Shelton Place. Polly Ann Shelton married Tim Hawkins in 1898. They not only had a hand dug well but they had also put up a retaining wall to pool some of the water from a spring. By pooling up the spring water they may have used it to help keep their food cool even in the summer. Can you imagine living out here with no electricity? No refrigerator, TV, phone, washer and dryer, electric drills, pumps, etc. How were they able to get by? Just past the old home site you can see another wall made of rocks off the trail to the right.

The trail now becomes a little steeper as we continue down hill and at 3.6 miles we come to **marker #15.** Here we can see two large red oak trees called "The Twins", one on each side of the trail. They seem to stand guard to the gate back to "civilization". The trees are about 24 inches in diameter and are estimated to be about 120 years old. That means that these two big oak trees were only little acorns around 1885 when this area was just being settled.

We now leave "The Twin" oaks and head down hill back to the steps at the trailhead.

Upon leaving the parking lot you can turn right and go back out the same way you came in or when you get to highway 248 at the end of Sycamore Log Church Road, you can turn to the right and go back to Branson and connect with Shepherd of the Hills Expressway and Gretna Road.

You can also exit to the left from the parking lot, going across the low water bridge, and follow the gravel road through the beautiful Roark Valley. The gravel road changes to Nolan road and then turns to blacktop after about one mile. At the top of the hill stay to the left as you go down hill to a stop sign. The road in front of you is highway 76.

If you turn right on highway 76 you can connect with highway 465 (Highroad), highway 265, Silver Dollar City or the town of Branson West.

If you turn left onto highway 76 you will go past the Shepherd of the Hills, Ruth and Paul Henning Forest Overlook and come to the junction of Shepherd of the Hills Expressway and highway 376 in Branson.

DEWEY BALD – HOMESTEAD TRAIL

For those of you who really want a challenge this is the trail for you! We will be hiking all five trails found in the Ruth and Paul Henning Conservation Area and by combining all five trails we will hike 6.8 miles and have an elevation change of about 500 feet.

Even though you can start your hike from either the trailhead off of highway 76 or the one on Sycamore Log Church Road we prefer to start at the trailhead on Sycamore Log Church Road. That way the first part of the hike is mainly uphill to the tower on the Dewey Bald Trail and the last half of the hike is downhill as we go back to Roark Creek.

DIRECTION TO TRAILHEAD

If you want to start the trail from the trailhead on Sycamore Log Church Road follow the directions to the Homestead Trail. To begin your hike from the highway 76 trailhead, follow the directions to the Dewey Bald Trail.

DESCRIPTION OF TRAIL

The description for this trail will be brief. For a more detailed explanation of each section go to the description for each individual trail as we come to that part of the trail. If you are looking at the maps we will be hiking these trails in a clockwise direction starting at the trailhead for the Homestead Trail. Locate the trail description for the Homestead Trail and follow its directions until we come to Shane's Shortcut Trail. Shane's Shortcut Trail will be on our left after passing marker #9 and crossing a wet weather creek at 1.6 miles.

Shane's Shortcut Trail will go up hill and along a couple of creeks then, it will turn to the right just before it comes to the Streamside Trail. Upon reaching the Streamside Trail take the trail to the left and the next trail we come to, at about 2.4 miles, is the Glade Trail.

Take the Glade Trail to the left. As we follow the Glade Trail it will take us up the side of the hill and at 2.7 miles we make a complete circle back to the beginning of the Glade Trail. We will take the trail to the left and come to the overlook at the highway 76 parking area. As we leave the overlook go left along the rock wall to the other end of the parking lot. Here we find some restrooms and the trailhead for the Dewey Bald Trail.

Take the paved trail up the hill until we come to the tower. If you have never been to the top now is the time. From up here you can see a lot of the city of Branson and the surrounding area. When you are ready, we will head back down the tower and follow the trail back to the overlook at the other end of the parking lot.

From the overlook take the steps down to the trail and go out through the woods until we come to a trail intersection at 3.8 miles. This time we will go to the left across the two wooden foot bridges. The trail will have woods on our left and SGV of the glade to our right. As we approach 4.2 miles we see another overlook deck with a bench! Take some time to rest and look around. I am so glad that the Henning's had the foresight to buy this land and the generosity to see that it ended up as a conservation area.

As we continue, follow the trail on around the deck and down the hill to the Streamside Trail at 4.5 miles. From here take the trail to the left, out through the woods and soon we will see Shane's Shortcut Trail on our left.

Follow the Shane's Shortcut back to the Homestead Trail. Upon connecting with the Homestead Trail, at 5.0 miles, take the trail to the left. Although it is not too bad, the trail does go up hill for awhile, out through the woods and then into an open glade. After we leave the glade we will go back into the woods, go under power lines and then back into the woods. This next section of the trail is fairly level as we are able to enjoy the quiet and peacefulness much like it was when the homesteaders lived on this land over a century ago.

We will soon come into another clearing as we go under more power lines. As the trail enters the woods on the other side we will see marker #13 on our left as we approach the 6.0 mile point of our hike. Continue to follow the Homestead Trail through the woods and down the hill until we come to the steps at the trailhead. Great job! You have just hiked 6.8 miles of some of the most scenic land in Taney County and burned about 3,300 calories.

Upon leaving the parking lot you can either go back to the right the way you came in or go to your left and this will take you out to highway 76. For more details see the last couple paragraphs of the Homestead Trail description.

SHEPHERD OF THE HILLS FISH HATCHERY

Just below Table Rock Dam, and the fish hatchery, there are several excellent hiking trails to choose from. Each trail can be accessed individually so you can hike each one separately for shorter hikes or combine them for a longer hike. Because of the shade and the cool water of Lake Taneycomo, the trails that follow along the lakes edge are good trails to hike on those hot summer days.

The three trails that follow along the edge of Lake Taneycomo are the White River Corridor Trail, the Canebrake Trail and the Fisherman's Trail. The White River Bluff Trail is just across the street and up the hill from the Canebrake trailhead. These trails lend themselves to being hiked as one big trail. You can park at the beginning of the White River Corridor Trail, hike it, continue on to the Canebrake Trail, and the Fisherman's Trail. Then on your way back, turn at the trailhead for the Canebrake trail, go across the road and hike the White River Bluff Trail then back across the street and continue on the White River Corridor Trail back to your car for a total hike of 3.3 miles. If you take the little side trails off of the White River Corridor Trail and Canebrake Trail, and/or explore along the lake's edge, you will add at least another 0.5 miles which will bring you to a total of about 3.8 miles. So, as you can see, you have all kinds of options. It just depends on how much hiking you want to do and how much time you have.

We will describe each trail separately, starting with the:

White River Corridor Trail
Canebrake Trail
Fisherman's Trail
White River Bluff Trail

That way if you want to hike each one separately you can. But if you do want to hike all the trails together all you have to do is follow each trails description as you come to them, starting with the White River Corridor Trail.

While you are here you need to plan enough time to visit

the fish hatchery. It is always a favorite with the kids. You can see a movie about how the fish are raised and then you can go and see the fish in the pools outside. They range from just inches in length up to several pounds. Be sure and bring along some quarters so you can buy some food and feed the fish!

Total miles hiked if you hike all trails together:

White River Corridor Trail	0.8
Canebrake Trail	0.7
Fisherman's Trail	0.4
White River Bluff Trail	1.4
Side Trails & River Edge	0.5
Total	3.8 miles

There is a little more distance hiked when you hike all the trails together as opposed to hiking each trail separately because there is about 0.1 mile distance between the end of the Canebrake Trail and the beginning of the Fisherman's Trail. So, we have added 0.1 mile to the mileage listed above on the Canebrake Trail.

WHITE RIVER CORRIDOR TRAIL 0.4 miles one way

GPS: N 36' 35.776   W 93' 18.215
Trail Length: 0.4 miles one way
Trail Type: Natural
Average Hiking Time: 30 - 45 minutes, one way
Rating: Easy, with some steps
Calories Burned: 160 – 230

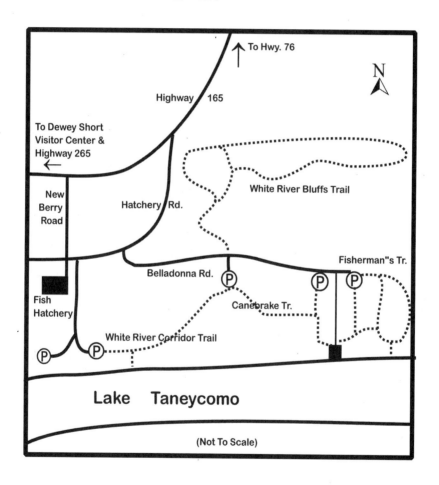

DIRECTIONS TO THE TRAILHEAD

From Branson, at the highway 65/76 junction, you have two options. You can take highway 76 west (out on the strip) for 3.2 miles and turn left onto highway 165. Go 3.6 miles and at the bottom of the hill turn left at the Dam and Fish Hatchery sign. Go about 0.1 miles to a stop sign. The fish hatchery parking lot will be right in front of you and Table Rock Dam will be on your right. We want to turn left at the stop sign, go about 50 feet and turn right on the paved road (no name) just past the fish hatchery parking lot. There will be a large fish pond on your left as you head down toward the lake. There will be a parking area on your left and on your right. If you can, park in the area to the left because the trailhead starts behind the pavilion on your left.

If traffic is backed up on highway 76 you can go south on highway 65 for 2.1 miles, turn right off of 65 and follow highway 165 across the dam. At the stop light, just past the dam, you will turn right and at the bottom of the hill, turn right at the Dam and Fish Hatchery sign and go to the stop sign. Then follow the same directions as above.

DESCRIPTION OF TRAIL

Before you start hiking you might take a few minutes to go down the wooden steps located between the two parking areas. If the water is low you can go down to the lakes edge. You will also see one of the places where the water from the fish hatchery discharges into Lake Taneycomo.

The trailhead for the White River Corridor Trail begins at the pavilion and starts off as concrete until you come to the first bridge. Just past the pavilion there is a rest room on your left and a trail description sign on your right. Sometimes there are some maps in a little metal box that you can get that shows the layout of the trail. If there are no maps, don't worry! We will describe the trail for you. As you can see on the sign there are several numbered posts along the way pointing out things of interest. These have been included in our trail description. Just past the sign you will see the trail split at **marker #1.**

The main trail will go to your left. The trail to your right is one of those little side trails we spoke of earlier.

On the trail to the right you will find a bench and some stairs. The stairs lead down to the lake. When the water level is low, this part of Lake Taneycomo looks much like it did before the dams were built on the White River. The water levels in this area change quite a bit. It all depends on how much rain there has been and how much power is being generated at the dam. If the water level is low this is a good place to explore. Take note, that if you hear a loud horn sounding, be sure and leave the waters edge and head back up to the trail. This is a warning that they are about to release more water from the dam and the water level can rise in a hurry. If the water level is already high be careful because the water will be swift and cold. Do not take any chances and be sure and watch your children!

To the left of the bench is a trail that leads out to a point where you can see more water being discharged from the fish hatchery and into the lake. You can also see the wooden bridge that we will be crossing in a few minutes.

Back on the main trail we will continue on to the right as we go across the wooden bridge. Here you will see **marker #2.** From the bridge you can see the creek below made by the water flowing from the fish hatchery back into the lake. The water is piped from the bottom of Table Rock Lake, flows through the hatchery, and then discharges at several points into Lake Taneycomo.

A little ways after you cross over the bridge you will see **marker #3** on your left. This is another side trail that goes up the steps to a viewing blind that overlooks a marshy area where you can watch birds and other wildlife. As you head up the steps notice the big sycamore tree at the bottom of the steps to your right. Then, toward the top of the steps, there will be a large oak tree straight ahead and a large walnut tree on the left. Be quiet as you approach the blinds, which is to the right after you get to the top of the steps, because you might get to see some wildlife in the area.

When you are ready head back and turn to the left at the

bottom of the steps. As we continue on the main trail we soon come to **marker #4.** From here you can see where a large sycamore tree has fallen into the lake. As with any river bank there is always the problem of erosion. When the dirt along the bank washes away it causes any plants and trees growing there to be washed away. This poor sycamore tree just couldn't hang on any longer. If you turn around you can see a large sycamore tree that is doing just fine, for now.

Soon we come to the second wooden bridge and **marker #5.** In the spring you can see the dogwood trees in bloom and in the summer and fall the orange blossoms of the touch-me-not plant is all around. The touch-me-not blossoms get there name because when the orange blossoms are touched they open up and the seeds pop out.

Continuing on the trail we come to **marker #6** and another wooden bridge. This bridge also has a bench at the end of it if you want to stop and rest awhile. Below the bridge is a little creek that usually doesn't run much water, unless it has been raining. We talked earlier about soil erosion, so while you are here, notice all the rocks, roots, leaves and plants in and along the creek that help to slow down the flow of water, thus, helping to prevent soil erosion.

The trail continues and we come to **marker #7.** Here we have a SGV of the lake. Just ahead, we will go up some wooden steps that give us more good views of the lake. On the way up there will be a bench on your left, then a walkway, up some more steps and then levels off.

At the end of the deck are two more benches where you can rest if you need to or if you just want to relax and enjoy the quiet. At the end of the deck you will see **marker #8.** From here you can see the lake below. During the winter, when the leaves are off the trees, it is even a better view. Behind you there are some railroad ties that leads up to the other end of the marshy area that we viewed at marker #3.

We are now walking on a level straight stretch of the trail and about in the middle of this section you will find **marker #9** on your right. In this area you will see a lot of May Apples growing along each side of the trail. They like to grow in shaded areas and usually bloom in May and the blossoms have a sweet smell. The white blossoms are about two inches in diameter and grow underneath the leaves. The fruit or "apple" usually ripens in late June and July and is edible and delicious, so we have been told. Janet and I have never eaten any so we just have to rely on what other people say. I did read where the roots, stems and leaves of the plant do contain toxins and is quite dangerous to eat but it is being used in cancer research. So don't eat the plant!

The trail turns to the right and we will go down twelve steps and follow the path along the edge of the lake. Soon you will hear the sound of running water. If you take the little trail down to the rivers edge you will see a beautiful water fall caused from the water that is being discharged from the fish hatchery.

Getting back on the main trail we come to **marker #10** and another SGV of the lake. If the water is low you will usually find several fly fishermen trying their skills at landing the big one! Also, be on the lookout for birds, turtles, lizards, butterflies and wild flowers.

After we go past marker #10 we will be going up twenty one steps. This brings us to another overlook at **marker #11.** This overlook is built along a small creek and if you happen to be here after a good rain there will be a small water falls to your left. You will find red bud trees and Pawpaw trees growing around the overlook area. The Pawpaw trees have long drooping leaves that grow up to twelve inches long. The flowers bloom for about six weeks during March through May depending on the weather. Each flower will produce several fruits, which when ripe, have a yellow flesh that is custard like and edible. Each fruit is about 3-6 inches in length and ripen over a four week period between the middle of August into October. The green fruit will lighten in color as it ripens and usually develops black splotches that do not affect the taste of the fruit. Inside are usually two rows of 10 to 14 seeds. Strips of bark from the Pawpaw tree was used by the Indians to make fabric and nets. As with the May Apples, Pawpaw leaves and twigs contain substances that are being researched for anticancer and pesticide uses. So don't eat the tree! Just the fruit!

When leaving the overlook take the trail up the hill (may be partially grown over) to **marker #12** which is another observation area. Watch out for the poison ivy growing around marker #12! This pond is usually dry except after a good rain or when they release water into it. But, if you are quiet and patient, you may still see a few birds and butterflies. We did see some beautiful morning glories blooming.

The trail will go along the fence, turn to the right, down some steps and back into the woods. We will come to another wooden bridge at **marker #13.** The creek that runs under the bridge is what feeds the water falls at the overlook we just came from. Just past this bridge the trail splits and this is the end of the White River Corridor Trail and the beginning of the Canebrake Trail. The trail to the left leads up to a parking area which is the trailhead for the White River Bluff Trail.

If you do turn around and follow the trail back to your car you will have hiked 0.8 miles if you stayed on the main trail. If you took the side trails you will have hiked about 1.2 miles and used 175 calories.

But if you want to continue hiking stay on the trail straight ahead and follow the Canebrake Trail.

CANEBRAKE TRAIL

0.3 miles one way

GPS:	N 36′ 35.910 W 93′ 17.881
Trail Length:	0.3 miles one way
Trail Type:	Natural
Average Hiking Time:	30 minutes one way
Rating:	Easy
Calories Burned:	160 one way

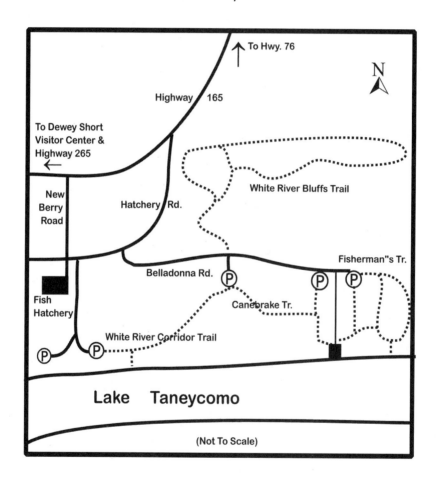

DIRECTIONS TO TRAILHEAD

From Branson, at the highway 65/76 junction, you have two options. You can take highway 76 west (out on the strip) for 3.2 miles and turn left onto highway 165. Go 3.6 miles and at the bottom of the hill turn left at the Dam and Fish Hatchery sign. Go about 0.1 miles to a stop sign. The fish hatchery parking lot will be right in front of you and Table Rock Dam will be on your right. We want to turn left at the stop sign, go about 0.1 mile and turn right onto Belladonna Trail road and the trailhead will at the parking lot on your right at 0.3 miles. The trailhead starts at the back of the parking lot.

If traffic is backed up on highway 76 you can go south on highway 65 for 2.1 miles, turn right off of 65 and follow highway 165 across the dam. At the stop light, just past the dam, you will turn right and at the bottom of the hill, turn right at the Dam and Fish Hatchery sign and go to the stop sign. Then follow the same directions as above.

DESCRIPTION OF TRAIL

If you are starting this trail from the parking lot enter the woods at the back and left of the parking lot and then turn left at the sign pointing to the Canebrake Trail. If you are continuing on from the White River Corridor Trail just follow the trail straight ahead from the White River Corridor Trail.

The trail will go down some wooden steps and there will be a sign on our left that shows a map of the trail. Next, we cross a small wooden foot bridge and during spring and summer there are usually some May apple plants along the trail. (For information on May Apples see the description in the White River Corridor Trail)

The trail goes slightly uphill to the right and crosses two more small wooden foot bridges. Just before the second foot bridge you will find a small field to your left. If you want, take a couple of minutes and look around. When you are ready, continue on across the second foot bridge where the trail goes slightly up hill, across a power line right of way, and then begins to descend and we will come to four steps. As you are going down the steps take notice of the big oak tree to your right. This tree has been here for centuries. The trail turns to the left and we are now hiking along the edge of the lake.

On your right you will notice a lesser trail that heads down to the lake. If the lake is low you can go and explore if you want to but beware that the trail gets pretty steep toward the bottom. When you get down to the river bed, look to your right and check to see if any water is running out of the ravine. If there is, you will find a little waterfall about 60-70 feet back up the ravine. Just take note that it will be muddy! If you are not sure about taking this side trail that's ok, there is a better place to access the lake's edge at the end of the trail.

Also, if you do go down to the lakes edge be aware that if you hear a loud horn sounding get back up to the trail quickly. This is a warning that water is about to be released from the dam for power production and the lake level can rise quickly. If the lake level is up don't get into the water because the current can be strong and the water very cold.

If you happen to be here when the lake level is low you are

probably seeing the river much like it was before the dam was built. But no matter what time of the day or the year you are here it is always beautiful along the lake. You can usually see a lot of different types of birds (if you're lucky you may even see a Bald Eagle), spot a beaver or a mink, see a fish jumping or watch a fly fisherman catch a rainbow trout.

As we go through the next section of the trail we will see cane growing on both sides of the trail, thus the name, Canebrake Trail. The trail remains level for awhile then turns and goes downhill as we get closer to the lake. It levels off for awhile then it will turn to the left and go up several wooden steps where we find a bench at the top. As you are going up the steps notice the wild grapevines, on your right, growing up the trees. After the bench, the trail will continue to wind along the edge of the lake.

A short distance further up the trail we will see a cylinder concrete tower on the right and a small metal shed on the left. The concrete tower is used to monitor the lake levels and the metal shed is a storage building.

If you follow the lesser trail down past the concrete tower to the waters edge you see the dam to your right and a large sycamore tree on your left with its roots exposed, trying to hold on a little longer.

Just past the tower, on the right, is a depth gauge nailed to a board attached to a tree. Believe me, if the water level gets this high we shouldn't be here!

A few feet ahead, at the sycamore tree, the trail will split and this is the end of the Canebrake Trail. The trail to the left leads to a parking lot. The trail to the right goes down along the edge of the lake and comes out at the boat ramp just ahead. This is the place we mentioned earlier as being a good place to access the edge of the lake.

If you turn around and go back to the Canebrake Trailhead you will have hiked 0.6 miles and burned about 80 calories. If you did take the side trails to the lake add another 0.2 miles and 30 more calories.

If you want to continue hiking take the trail to the right past a large sycamore tree and down some steps to the boat ramp. Take awhile to look around and enjoy the lake. When you are ready to continue go up the boat ramp and turn right at the top of the hill. This will take you to the trailhead for the Fisherman's Trail.

FISHERMAN'S TRAIL

0.4 mile loop

GPS: N 36' 35.868 W 93' 17.589
Trail Length: 0.4 miles loop
Trail Type: Natural
Average Hiking Time: 30 minutes
Rating: Easy
Calories Burned: 160

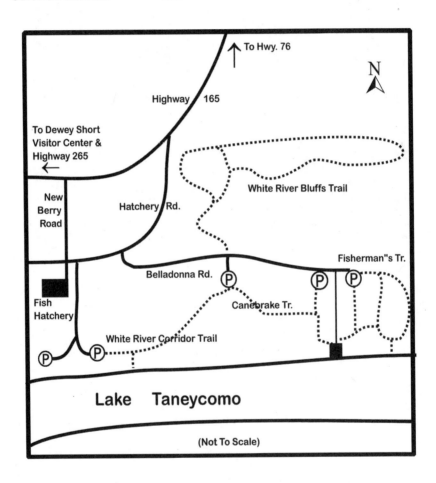

DIRECTIONS TO TRAILHEAD

From Branson, at the highway 65/76 junction, you have two

options. You can take highway 76 west (out on the strip) for 3.2 miles and turn left onto highway 165. Go 3.6 miles and at the bottom of the hill turn left at the Dam and Fish Hatchery sign. Go about 0.1 miles to a stop sign. The fish hatchery parking lot will be right in front of you and you can see Table Rock Dam on your right. We want to turn left at the stop sign, go about 0.1 mile and turn right onto Belladonna Trail road and go past the boat ramp to the end of the road at 0.6 miles. The trail-head starts in the field straight across the parking lot.

If traffic is backed up on highway 76 you can go south on highway 65 for 2.1 miles, turn right off of 65 and follow highway 165 across the dam. At the stop light, just past the dam, you will turn right and at the bottom of the hill, turn right at the Dam and Fish Hatchery sign and go to the stop sign. Then follow the same directions as above.

DESCRIPTION OF TRAIL

We will begin the trail by walking through the small field at the end of the parking lot. Be on the look out for a rabbit or two. After about 0.1 miles the trail will turn to the right and head into the woods. Right in front of you the trail splits and you will be a sign showing a map of the trail. As you can see this trail loops around and comes out on the other end. Let's begin by taking the trail to the right.

The trail starts off being pretty level as it winds itself through the woods. Then we come to some railroad tie steps that take us down toward the lake. At the bottom of the steps we will go to our left. Now, look to your right for a SGV of the lake. If you head down the trail to the lake you will be able to see Table Rock Dam to your right. Across the lake is the KOA campground that is accessed off of highway 165 across from the State Park. The upper end of Lake Taneycomo is a favorite place for trout fisherman, especially those that fly fish.

Just a short distance up the main trail there will be a large sycamore tree on the right and some wooden steps that take us down to the lake. This is another SGV. If the water level is low spend some time looking around and watching the fisherman catch some fish. Do you see any fish swimming around?

The trail continues to go along the edge of the river bank. A little ways up the trail, to the left, you will see some more railroad tie steps. There is a trail that goes straight ahead, which you can explore if you want to but it doesn't go very far. When you are ready follow the trail up the steps. One spring day, when we hiked this trail, the weeds and grass had taken over the steps. Hope you remembered to put on some bug spray!

At the top of the stairs the main trail will turn and go to the left. There is a trail that goes to the right which follows along the lake and ends up at the Point Royal Subdivision. But this part of the trail has been closed by the Missouri Department of Conservation, they say for safety reasons. So we will continue our hike by taking the trail to the left.

Before you know it we are back at the sign where we started the trail. Take the trail back to the left, the same way we went earlier, and follow it back down to the bottom of the steps.

This time, when we get to the bottom of the steps, we will take the trail to the right. The trail will follow along the edge of the lake and across a wooden bridge. Right after the bridge we will go up more steps. Just as you get close to the top of the steps you will see a lesser trail take off to the left and the main trail will continue on up the steps. If you parked in the lot at the top of the boat ramp take the trail on up the steps back to your car.

But if you are hiking several of these trails together and are parked at the beginning of the Canebrake Trail or the White River Corridor Trail you will want to take the trail to the left.

You will follow this trail through the woods, across the boat ramp, and back into the woods to the Canebrake Trail. You can follow the trail back to your car or if you want to hike the White River Bluff Trail while you are here go back to the beginning of Canebrake Trail. When the Canebrake Trail and the White River Corridor Trail meet turn to the right up to the parking lot. Go across the parking lot to the trailhead across the road.

Three of anything is a recognized sign of distress. Whistles, shots, yells, etc.

WHITE RIVER BLUFF TRAIL

1.4 miles

GPS:	N 36' 35.910 W 93' 17.881
Trail Length:	1.4 mile loop
Trail Type:	Natural
Average Hiking Time:	1 hour
Rating:	Moderate
Calories Burned:	460

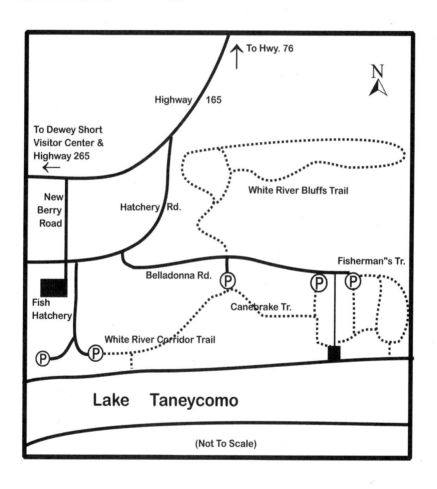

DIRECTIONS TO TRAILHEAD

From Branson, at the highway 65/76 junction, you have two options. You can take highway 76 west (out on the strip) for 3.2 miles and turn left onto highway 165. Go 3.6 miles and at the bottom of the hill turn left at the Dam and Fish Hatchery sign. Go about 0.1 miles to a stop sign. The fish hatchery parking lot will be right in front of you and Table Rock Dam will be on your right. We want to turn left at the stop sign, go about 0.1 mile and turn right onto Belladonna Trail road and the trailhead will at the parking lot on your right at 0.3 miles. The trailhead starts across the road from the parking lot.

If traffic is backed up on highway 76 you can go south on highway 65 for 2.1 miles, turn right off of 65 and follow highway 165 across the dam. At the stop light, just past the dam, you will turn right and at the bottom of the hill, turn right at the Dam and Fish Hatchery sign and go to the stop sign. Then follow the same directions as above.

DESCRIPTION OF TRAIL

The sign at the beginning of the trail says the trail is 1.3 miles in length. But each time we have hiked the trail we come up with 1.4 miles. There is a trail book from the Missouri Department of Conservation that also lists the trail as 1.4 miles. So we have listed it as 1.4 miles. This trail has been changed some over the years.

We begin on the other side of the road from the parking lot and head into a small field then left into the woods. After the trail gets into the woods it will turn to the right and begin to go slightly uphill.

Soon we are going through a small grove of pine trees. Be sure and notice the big pine tree on your left. Pine trees are not only beautiful but they were also a great source of lumber for the early settlers.

At 0.1 miles we come to a "Y" in the trail. We will go to the left. The trail on the right is the way we will be coming back. The trail will continue to wind its way uphill, across a small glade and over some ledge rock as we go through the woods.

If you are starting to get a little tired, we will be coming to a bench on the left side of the trail. Stop and rest a few minutes if you want to. The trail right behind the bench just leads up to a few houses, so, when you are ready, we will go straight ahead on the main trail.

Just past the bench, at 0.3 miles, we will come to another trail intersection. The trail to the right connects to the trail that we will use on our way back. If, for some reason, you do want to go back to your car at this point go straight ahead and then take the trail to the right back down the hill to the trail-head. You will have hiked 0.5 miles on this trail. But for the rest of us we will take the trail to the left and follow it on uphill.

We will be crossing over a couple of small wooden foot bridges as we continue to wind our way uphill through the woods. Then at 0.5 miles the trail opens up into a small opening and it levels off as we go across the top of the hill. Just past the small clearing we will come to a sign that points the way to Gerth's campground and the Point Royale subdivision. These are accessed off of highway 165 as you go back to Branson from the fish hatchery. We will continue to follow the trail to the right of the sign.

Not far ahead, the trail opens up as we go through some cedar trees and glades. Glade areas are always interesting; you never know what you will find. You may see flowers, butter-flies, birds, lizards, turkeys, deer, rock formations or any number of other things that might catch your attention. Be quiet and look around.

After the trail leaves the glade it enters back into the woods and we find another bench on our right. This next part of the trail is level and is a very nice hike through the Ozark forest. There are several big, old oak trees. Some are still standing, others have fallen over and others are just trying to make it. These trees have been here for centuries. There is an interesting tree formation that will be on the right side of the trail. Three trees are growing right beside each other as if growing from the same root system. The tree in the center is a huge old oak tree and on either side of it are a cedar tree and a sweet gum tree.

At 0.8 miles you will see a sign where the trail comes to a "T". The trail to the left opens up into a small field and goes into the Point Royale subdivision. Go and have a look around if you want to but then come back and we will continue on the trail that goes to the right.

Just ahead, on the left, is a lesser trail that also goes into the Point Royal subdivision but has been closed by the Missouri Department of Conservation. So we will keep going straight on the main trail.

Be sure and look to your left, through the leaves during the summer, and catch glimpses of the hills on the other side of Lake Taneycomo. In the fall and early winter this is really a view of the Ozark hills.

We will go through another small glade, down across ledge rock before we head back uphill slightly and back into the woods. This section of the trail continues to gradually go up and down and in and out of the glades and woods as we hike across the side of the hill.

As we approach the 1.2 mile point we go down over more ledge rock and across two wooden foot bridges. Just past the bridges we come to a trail intersection. We want to go downhill to our left as we go back to the trailhead. If you continue

straight ahead you will be back on the main trail where we
were earlier.

At 1.3 miles we connect with the main trail. We want to go
to the left on down the hill to the trailhead at 1.4 miles.

If you parked in the parking lot across the road you are
finished. But if you are parked back at the trailhead of the
Whiter River Corridor Trail you will need to go across the road,
into the woods on the other side, turn right and follow the trail
back to your car.

MISSOURI STATE PARKS

Interest in developing a state park system began to be discussed in the early 1900's. Although it did not pass, the first bill to establish a state park system was introduced in the Missouri General Assembly in 1907. Then, in 1914, a committee of six senators spent four days traveling around the state to look at proposed sites to be purchased for use as state parks.

In 1916 the National Park Service was created which also help the states establish their own park systems. So, in 1917 the Missouri legislature passed a law establishing a state park fund with money from the fish and game department. But it wasn't until October, 17, 1924 that Missouri got its first state park, Big Spring State Park.

By the end of 1925 Missouri had eight tracks of land totaling 23,244 acres. The park system continued to grow and by 1932 Missouri had eighteen state parks with more than 500,000 visitors a year.

Throughout the years the Missouri State Park system was funded in various ways. Then, in 1984, Missouri voters stood behind their commitment to the park system by passing a one-tenth-of-one-percent sales tax that would be equally divided between the State Park system and soil and water conservation efforts in Missouri. This taxed was renewed in 1988 and in 1996.

Today, the Missouri State Park system is made up of nearly 138,000 acres in more than 80 different areas throughout the state. Did you know that 60% of the land in the Missouri State Park System has been donated?

For more information on what to do and where to go in Missouri's State Parks visit their home page at mostateparks.com. If you want to learn more about the history of Missouri State Park system go to: *mostateparks.com/history.htm*.

"If you are seeking creative ideas, go out walking. Angels whisper to a man when he goes for a walk."
Raymond Inmon

TABLE ROCK LAKE STATE PARK

Table Rock State Park is just one of many beautiful parks located throughout the state of Missouri. It is made up of 356 acres right along the shores of Table Rock Lake. There are two camping areas that range from basic to electric/sewer/water hook-ups, restrooms, showers and laundry rooms. A public marina provides everything you need for and enjoyable time on the lake. There is a dive shop, you can rent ski boats, pontoon boats, personal water craft, fishing boats and all the supplies that go along with a great day on the lake. You can hike, swim, go on a picnic and you can even go parasailing or take an excursion on a 48 foot catamaran. For more information call 417.334.4704.

There are three trails in the park, Juniper Trail, Chinquapin Trail and the newest one is the Table Rock Lakeshore Trail. To be honest with you I thought there were only two trails in the park until one day when I was talking with one of the park attendants about getting a sign put up for the trailhead to the Chinquapin Trail, which I thought started at the parking lot of the Park Office. Instead, I was informed, that even though there are no signs, the trail between the Park Office and the Amphitheater was the Juniper Trial. The Chinquapin Trail Started at the Amphitheater and connected with the Table Rock Lakeshore Trail, now I know. I did request that some signs be put up that would identify the Juniper Trail and they said they would let my request be known. We will see what happens.

All three of these trails are point to point trails, although the Chinquapin Trial does have a little loop at the end. We will describe each trail separately, but if you would like, you can combine the trails for a longer hike. The Juniper Trail and the Chinquapin Trail is a natural to be linked together for a 2.1 mile hike. As I said earlier, I thought it was one trail anyway. Or, if you wanted to, you could hike the Juniper Trail, Chinquapin Trail and then the Table Rock Lakeshore Trail for a hike of 6.4 miles.

Since the completion of the **Table Rock Lakeshore Trail**

in the fall of 2004, the Chinquapin Trail and Juniper Trail haven't seen as much use, so be sure and give them a try. All three of these trails are excellent for those with younger children or just want an easy hike with some beautiful scenery.

CHINQUAPIN TRAIL

1.3 miles

GPS: N 36' 34.874   W 93' 18.178
Trail Length: 1.3 mile loop
Trail Type: Natural
Average Hiking Time: 45 minutes – 1 hour
Rating: Easy
Calories Burned: 230 – 310

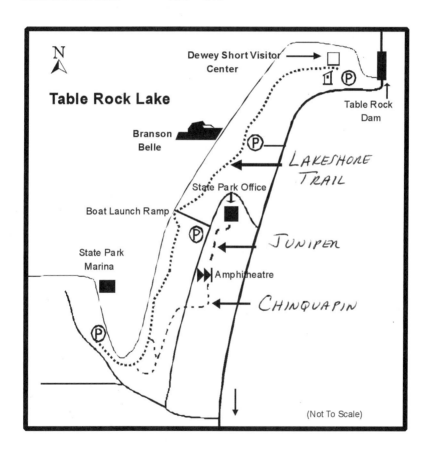

The trail is named for a type of oak tree, the Chinquapin oak. (Chin-ka-pin) Take note that this trail does cross one of the roads in the park so be sure to look both ways and watch your children as you go across. There are also some wet weather streams so if you happen to be here just after a good rain you will get you feet wet but there will also be some beautiful views and good photo opportunities. This trail has been changed by the development of the Table Rock Lakeshore Trail. It originally went on up to campground #2, which you can still take if you want. When you get to the wooden bridge on the Table Rock Lakeshore Trail go to the left and go about 0.1 miles and you will see a trail on the left that will leave the paved trail, go uphill across two roads and comes out at the campground. But the trail, as we will describe it, will go to the right at the wooden bridge and follow the paved Table Rock Lakeshore Trail for awhile then back in the woods. Once you know your way around feel free to explore all you want.

DIRECTIONS TO TRAILHEAD

Follow the same directions as described for the Juniper Trail.

DESCRIPTION OF TRAIL

As you come into the parking lot you will see the sign for the trailhead on your right. Stay to the right of the ramp that goes up to the east side of the Amphitheater and there will be a sign that says Chinquapin Trail 0.5 miles with a blue and green arrow. Hike past the sign, across the paved service road and into the glade and cedar trees. Off to your right you can see campground #1.

We will hike out through the woods and at 0.2 miles the trail crosses the road. Be sure and look both ways before crossing the road and keep an eye on the kids. We will be going down the wooden steps that are off to our left. After we go down the steps the trail will go down hill then turn to the left then back to the right as we cross a wet weather creek. Notice the ledge rock on our left.

A short distance ahead at 0.4 miles we come to a sign post and the trail splits, green trail to the left and blue trail to the right. We will follow the green arrow and go to the left. The trail will go slightly uphill and to the right. You will see a lesser trail to the left but we want to stay to the right, going through some small glades. The trail will follow along the road and wind around through the trees and across the top of ledge rock. The rocks can be slippery so watch your step.

We will come upon another wet weather creek and the trail will turn to the right, going slightly downhill. This area is really beautiful if you happen to be here just after a hard rain. The trail will now follow along the edge of the creek and we will come out at one of the wooden bridges on the Table Rock Lakeshore Trail. This is the end of the green section of the trail.

We will now go to the right as we follow the paved Table Rock Lakeshore Trail. The water you see on your left is a cove on Table Rock Lake where the State Park Marina is located. As you go around the next curve there will be another wooden bridge up ahead. Look to your right and locate a blue mark on a tree. This is where we go back into the woods and follow the blue section of the trail back to the sign post at 0.8 miles. When you reach the post be sure and go to the left and follow the trail back to the trailhead for a hike of 1.3 miles.

JUNIPER TRAIL

0.8 miles

GPS:	N 36' 34.874 W 93' 18.178
Trail Length:	0.8 round trip
Trail Type:	Natural
Average Hiking Time:	30 – 45 minutes
Rating:	Easy
Calories Burned:	160 – 230

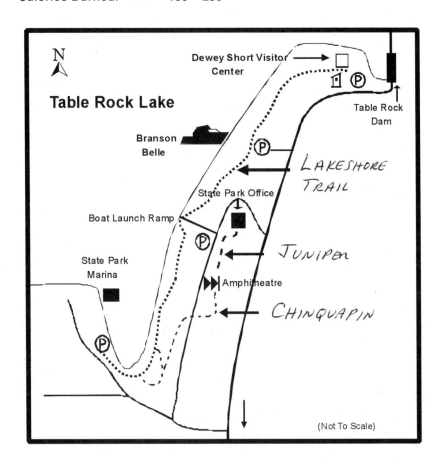

Directions to Trailhead

There are a couple of ways you can go. One way is from the highway 76/65 overpass go west on highway 76 for 3.2 miles and at the stoplight turn left onto highway 165. You will follow highway165 all the way out to Table Rock Dam. After crossing the dam go about one mile and turn right into the Table Rock State Park. Go around the Park Office building and turn left at the stop sign. Going straight through the intersection go 0.5 miles where you will see the Amphitheater on your left. This is the trailhead for both the Juniper Trail and Chinquapin Trail. The second way to get there is to go south on highway 65 from the highway 76/65 junction in Branson and go about 2.5 miles and turn right at the interchange in Hollister. Follow the signs to College of the Ozarks and at the college entrance go left and go about 6.0 miles and turn left into Table Rock State Park then follow the directions as described above.

DESCRIPTION OF TRAIL

The trail begins by following the path up to the Amphitheater. Then go to the left around the seats and follow the trail out through the woods. If the Amphitheater is in use go to the left of the Amphitheater and connect with the trail at the back of the seats.

The trail will wind its way through the cedar trees and bushes. It is easy to follow and seems secluded even though we are just yards from a road on each side of the trail. Be on the lookout for birds, lizards, chipmunks, squirrels, beautiful flowers and whatever else you can find.

When we get to about the half way point the trail will open up into a glade. The trail will go along the right side of the glade and is not as well defined through this section. If you look to your left you can see glimpses of Table Rock Lake. As we get to the other side of the glade the trail will turn to the right, go into the woods and you can see where rocks have been lined up along the sides of the trail. The trail will go up hill slightly and turn to the left as we go around a cedar tree that has some odd growth rings around it. To the right you will see a bird house attached to a post.

The trail will across a small clearing then back into the woods for a short distance and we will see more rocks lined up along the trail as we come to the end of the trail at the parking lot of the Park Office building. If it is hot outside you might want to go inside and cool off. When ready turn around and follow the trail back to the Amphitheater for a hike of 0.8 miles.

TABLE ROCK LAKESHORE TRAIL   4.4 miles

GPS:	N 36' 35.216 W 93' 17.314
Trail Length:	4.4 miles round trip
Trail Type:	Paved
Average Hiking Time:	2 hours
Rating:	Easy
Calories Burned:	620

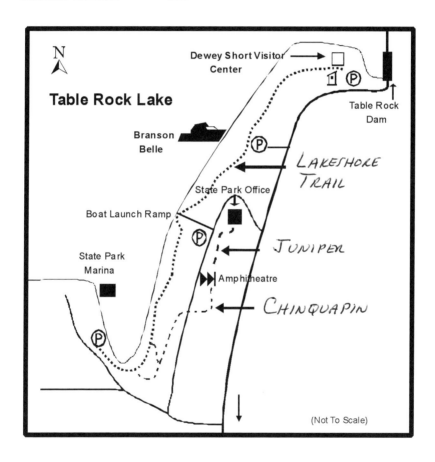

This trail was finished in the fall of 2004 at a cost of about $500,000.00 and was built with the cooperation of the U.S. Army Corps of Engineers, Missouri Department of natural

Resources and the Herschend Family Entertainment Corp. (Silver Dollar City). It is a beautiful, paved trail with very little elevation changes as it winds along the shores of Table Rock Lake. It is a multi-use trail for walking, jogging, and bicycles with beautiful lake views, a picnic area and restrooms. It is a great place to pack a lunch and spend the day. We use this trail quite a bit for hiking and biking. We often take the grand-kids with us and they really enjoy it. The first time we took our five year old granddaughter biking with us we weren't sure she could make it the whole 4.4 miles of the trail, but she did. In fact, when we were finished she wanted to go again! So take the kids, the grandkids, or someone else's kids, but go and enjoy this easy and beautiful trail.

One thing to keep in mind is that if you are hiking on a hot day you might want to take advantage of the air conditioning inside the Dewey Short Visitor Center. After you get cooled off go back outside and take the sidewalk that leads to the dam where you will have a SGV of both lakes, Table Rock and Taneycomo. You do have to cross the road at the dam to see the Lake Taneycomo side so be sure and hold onto the kids. Also, at the front of the visitor center, are some steps that led down to the lake for another SGV. You can go all the way around the edge of the lake to your left and it will connect back with the Table Rock Lakeshore Trail.

DIRECTIONS TO TRAILHEAD

There are several places you can access the trail. You can begin from the State Park Marina, behind the State Park office, the Showboat Branson Belle parking lot (when open during season), or from the Dewey Short Visitor Center. Toward the middle of the trail at the State Park Office there is a boat ramp and picnic area with bar-b-que grills where you could park, walk or ride the trail in both directions and they enjoy a cook out when you are finished!

We are going to start the trail from the Dewey Short Visitor Center so from the highway 76/65 overpass go west on highway 76 for 3.2 miles and turn left onto highway 165. Follow 165 for about 5.5 miles and just as you go over Table Rock Dam you will see the entrance to the Dewey Short Visitor Center on your right. The trailhead begins at the back corner of the parking lot to the left of the visitor center and to the right of the restrooms.

If you do want to start at one of the other access points just continue on past the entrance to the Dewey Short Visitor Center. The next entrance you come to will be the Showboat Branson Belle. Just pull into their parking lot and the trail begins in the yellow stripped pedestrian lane marked on the pavement in front of the entrance.

The next access point is the State Park Office building. Turn right into the park, go around the park office and turn left at the stop sign. From here you can park just about anywhere. You can take the first road to the right and this will take you to the boat ramp with several places to park. Or go past the boat ramp road and you will see a couple of smaller parking lots to your right. The trail runs between the parking lots and the lake.

The other end of the trail begins at the State Park Marina. You will turn right onto State Park Marina Street, go straight through the first intersection and then stay to the right at the "Y". The parking lot and trailhead will be on your right.

DESCRIPTION OF TRAIL

Let's begin at the trailhead to the right of the restrooms. The trail is paved and easy to walk. A few yards down the trail you will see a walkway to your right. This will take you along the edge of the lake around the visitor center and has a SGV of the lake. If you want to you can take this path on your return trip. For now we will continue on the trail as it turns to your left. As you walk through this section of the trail you can still see the remains of the old walking path that looped through the woods before the paved trail was built.

At 0.3 miles, on your left, you come to the first bench that you will find on the trail.

Next at 0.6 miles the trail opens up to the RV parking lot for the Showboat Branson Belle. If you do have small children be sure and watch them through this section. Even though you will be walking in a pedestrian yellow stripped walkway, there are cars and RV's traveling in this area. Stay in the walkway as you go across the lot and just after you pass the archway that leads down to the Branson Belle the trail turns to the right on the paved path. There are some beautiful trees in this next part of the trail.

At 0.8 miles the trail crosses a ramp that the Ducks use to access the lake. These are WWII amphibious boats used for riding tours, not birds! So be sure and look both ways before crossing the ramp. The Ducks usually blow there horn before they cross the trail.

Then at 0.9 miles you come to another bench located on your left.

At 1.1 miles you will come upon a boat launching ramp. Just before you cross the boat ramp on your left are RESTROOMS! It is a small wooden building that looks like a cabin. If you do have small children you will probably need it about now! After using the restrooms we will now cross the boat ramp, being careful to hold on to the kids and watching for cars.

Continue on across the boat ramp and there you will find some more benches. The trail also changes to concrete and is a little narrower.

The next thing you will see at 1.3 miles is the picnic tables and bar-b-que grills. A lot of people also use this area for fishing and swimming. Stay to the right as the trail turns and goes around the cove. On your right are a couple of benches that are usually in the shade and have a SGV of the lake. Even if you are not tired you might want to just stop and enjoy the view!

The trail continues on around the cove and through the woods. At 1.7 miles there will be another bench on your right.

As the trail winds around the cove, at 1.9 miles, you will see a camping area on your left and some more great views of the lake on your right.

At 2.0 miles you come to the first of two wooden bridges on the trail. The second bridge is up ahead at 2.1 miles.

Finally, you will be at the parking lot and trailhead at the

State Park Marina end of the trail. You have hiked 2.2 miles. Just turn around and follow the path back to the visitor center for a total hike of 4.4 miles. If you hike up to the dam and around the visitor center you can add another 0.6 miles to your hike for a total of 5.0 miles.

"Perhaps the truth depends on a walk around the lake."

Wallace Stevens

U.S. DEPARTMENT OF AGRICULTURE - NATIONAL FOREST

On February 1,1905, President Theodore Roosevelt signed a bill that established the Forest Service as an agency of the U.S Department of Agriculture. At that time there were about 63 million acres of forest and grasslands. Today, over 100 years later, the Forest Services oversees about 193 million acres of National Forest and grasslands, which is about the size of Texas. On September 3, 1964, President Lyndon B. Johnson signed the Wilderness Act of 1964. This was done to secure and protect lands for the American people of present and future generations. Wilderness areas are set aside to preserve some of the country's last remaining wild places so that they will be protected from development and can retain their natural processes.

The 8,142 acre Piney Creek Wilderness Area was set aside as a Wilderness Area on December 22, 1980. It is located in parts of Barry and Stone counties and is part of the Mark Twain National Forest. Some of the ridge tops rise more than 400 feet above its main creek, Piney Creek, which flows into the James River Arm of Table Rock Lake.

The area is covered mostly with Oak and Hickory trees, along with pines, sycamore, ash, walnut and eastern cedar. In the spring you will see redbuds and dogwoods along with many beautiful wildflowers. During the summer months everything is green and in the fall you can enjoy the brilliant colors provided by the many different species of trees and plants.

For more information on this area you can call the Cassville Office at 417.847.2144 or write to P.O. Box 310, Cassville, Mo. 65625.

"An early morning walk is a blessing for the whole day."
Henry David Thoreau

FIRE TOWER TRAIL

4.2 miles

GPS: N 36' 35.597   W 93' 18.892
Trail Length: 4.2 mile Loop
Trail Type: Natural
Average Hiking Time: 4.5 hours
Rating: Difficult
Calories Burned: 2,070

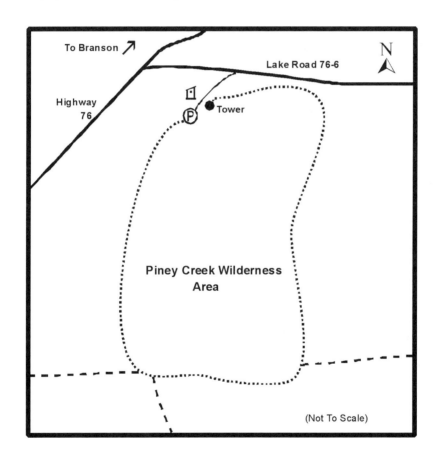

This area is about an hour drive from downtown Branson. There are 8,142 acres in the Piney Creek Wilderness. The brochure says there are about 13.1 miles of trails but I could not find any reference to the distance of the individual different trails so Janet and I used our pedometers to come up with the distance for this section of the trail. Take yours along and see what you come up with. On this trail you will be challenged with some rough descents, steep inclines, and during wet weather, some muddy sections where the horses have torn up the trail. Even though these rough sections do not last very long you need to be in good hiking shape. This is not a trail for the novice hiker, children or people with heart problems. There is no place to get water so be sure and bring plenty with you, especially when it is hot, you will need it. There is a restroom to your right when you come into the parking lot and there are also a few picnic tables around the edge of the parking area.

DIRECTIONS TO TRAILHEAD

From Branson you will drive about 36.5 miles and it will take you about an hour. Go north on highway 65 from the highway 76/65 junction go 7 miles and get off at the highway 160 exit. Go left onto highway 160 toward Reeds Spring Jct.

Stay on highway 160 for 9 miles and you will come to a stop sign at highway 13. Go left on highway 13 for 2.8 miles and turn right onto highway 76. (Yes, this is the same 76 that goes through Branson) Follow highway 76 straight through the stop light. After another 7 miles (26 miles from Branson) you will go through some sharp S curves and will come out on the James River Arm of Table Rock Lake at Cape Fair. After you cross over the bridge there is a gas station on your left where you can get gas, snacks & water for the hike, use the restrooms or just stretch your legs.

Continue going west on highway 76 through Cape Fair. In town there will be a **SHARP** curve to the right go about 0.5 miles and turn to the left at the junction of highway 76 and 173. Be sure and turn left as we continue to follow highway 76. After about 6 miles from Cape Fair (33 total miles from Branson) you will see highway EE on your right. Go on past highway EE for another 2.5 miles (35.5 miles from Branson) and turn left onto Lake Road 76-6. Go another mile and turn right onto the gravel road which leads to the fire tower and trailhead.

DESCRIPTION OF TRAIL

Use the restroom, put on bug spray, get your camera, snacks, water and let's begin! The trailhead begins at the back side of the parking lot past the fire tower. After about 0.1 mile on your right you can see a foundation of an old building and what looks like could have been a cistern. We continue out through the woods along the top of the ridge.

At 0.5 the trail gets pretty steep as it heads down hill over some large rocks. Through the trees you can see the valley below and soon the trail opens up into a small glade on your left. Just past the glade the trail will split. Stay to the left as both trails will come back together.

At 0.7 we come to a small creek which may be dry during hot weather. The trail will continue up the hill on the other side of the creek.

This next section is steep and during wet weather, muddy, because the trail has been torn from the horses. Again, the trail splits but will soon come back together. The trail to the right doesn't seem to be as steep as the one on the left.

At 0.9 we come to a small glade at the top of the hill. Sit and rest a while! When you are ready continue following the trail on through the glade. This next section is an easy hike for the next mile or so, enjoy!

We will be hiking along the edge of a ridge with a valley to our right and some interesting ledge rock on our left. This trail is really beautiful in the fall with all of its many colors. Have you noticed how tall the mountain top is over to your right and the little wild flowers along the trail? The trail will gradually go down hill then gets a little steeper with some loose rocks as you get toward the bottom.

There will be a camp site on our left at 1.8 miles with Piney Creek in front of us. The trail will go straight across the creek. Should you be here just after a hard rain be careful because the creek can get pretty high. Don't take any chances, remember, help is a long way off! Since Piney Creek does have a few springs there is usually a little water running.

As we get to the other side of the creek you will see that the trail goes to your right and left, take the trail to your left. We will soon cross another little creek and once again when we get to the other side the trail splits. We will be taking the trail to the left. The trail continues through the bottom land but we do leave the creek for awhile. If you haven't put on any bug spray you might want to put some on before you go through this next section. We will be walking through a brushy area for awhile and is a good place for ticks and chiggers.

At 2.1 miles the trail will come back to the creek bottom, although not the main part of Piney Creek. When we get across the creek look to your left and see the biggest sycamore tree that I have ever seen. Janet and I measured around it about chest high and it was 14 feet! I wonder, how old is this tree?

At 2.3 miles we are back at Piney creek. There is a nice little pool of clear water. If you want to, take off your socks and shoes and cool your feet off for awhile. (I haven't been here in the middle of summer so I am not sure if there will be any water during that time of the year)

The trail leaves the creek for a short ways then at 2.4 miles we are back at the creek again. There is a trail that goes on across the creek and will take you about one mile to the edge of Table Rock Lake, but we will be taking the trail to the left.

We are now leaving the FLAT bottom land and will be continuing our journey UPWARD back to the trailhead. And I do mean upward. This is the toughest part of the trail. Fortunately, it doesn't last very long. As we go up the side of the hill, for about 0.2 miles, you will know what the difficult rating for this trail is all about. Just take your time and rest often.

After the trail loops around a tree look to your right look at the valley below and see how far you have climbed. Hang in there! We are almost to the top!

At 2.6 miles the trail begins to level off. We will still be going uphill but not nearly as steep. The worst is over!

For about the next mile the trail continues to gradually go

up and down as we follow the top of the ridge. There are many beautiful pine, oak, hickory, and cedar trees. There is a brushy area at about 3.5 miles. Not sure what happened, maybe there had been a fire or it could have been logged off. Whatever the reason, we are soon back in the middle of the mature trees.

At 3.7 miles we come to a small opening. There will be a trail that goes to our right but we want to stay on the trail that goes to the left. A little further ahead you will see some trails taking off in different directions. If you look on ahead you will see a paved road. This is 76-6 and will take you back up to the gravel road that leads back to the fire tower. But we want to stay to the left and take the trail that heads down a ravine then back up the other side. The trail will wind up the hill and at the top the trail splits. Take the trail to the right and we will come out into the parking lot and can see the tower on our left.

When you leave, turn left on 76-6 and then right onto highway 76. You can follow highway 76 all the way back into Branson, or you can go back the same way that you came.